The Flame of Love

The Renewal of the Earth Will Take Place Through the Power and Imploring Force of the Blessed Virgin Mary

~Our Lord to Elizabeth Kindelmann

Elizabeth Kindelmann

Nihil Obstat: Monsignor Joseph G. Prior
                  Censor Librorum

Imprimatur: Archbishop Charles Chaput
                 Archdiocese of Philadelphia

Printed in the United States of America

Contents

History of Flame of Love

Diary of Elizabeth Kindelmann

In 1962, our heavenly Mother gave us her Flame of Love. Father Gabriel Rona, S.J., now a resident of Budapest, Hungary, spent thirty years in Ecuador and translated this diary from Hungarian into Spanish. His Spanish translation was used for the newest English editions—the complete Spiritual Diary and this Simplified Version.

In June 1989, Cardinal Bernardino Echeverria Ruiz (Archdiocese of Guayaquil, Ecuador) approved the publication of Fr. Rena's translation. On October 22, 1996, he approved the statutes of the Flame of Love Movement and asked the Holy Father to give approval so that the Flame of Love would be accepted in the whole Church. Cardinal Echeverria Ruiz died on April 6, 2000, a great apostle of the Flame of Love.

The Vatican, through Cardinal Francis Stafford, responded to Fr. Rona for the Holy Father. "I encourage you to continue so the Association bears abundant fruits among its members and the whole Church. I invite you to continue your duties as spiritual director."

In 1983, this devotion arrived in Mexico and then spread to Canada and the United States. On June 5, 2009, Cardinal Peter Erdo, Archbishop of Esztegom, Budapest, Hungary, gave his imprimatur to the original Spiritual Diary.

Comments by Fr. Rona, S.J.

After suffering three years in the mystical trials of the "Dark Night," Our Lady brings Elizabeth back into the light. Then, by interior locutions, she hears Our Lord's and Our Lady's voices. In these locutions, Our Lady confronts Satan (her eternal enemy), who wants to ruin souls. She reveals that she has gained from her Son "an outpouring of graces so great that they have not existed since the Word became Flesh." This is her Flame of Love bursting forth from her Immaculate Heart by which she will blind Satan. The Blessed Virgin pleads and begs that we share in her work by our prayers, sacrifices, family holy hours and fasting.

What is new in this Diary? These writings show how the Blessed Virgin feels and acts now in our day. It reveals her divine Motherhood and her intense preoccupation with the salvation of her children's souls. Listen to her own words, "Take this Flame of Love of my Heart. Light your own heart and pass it on. With this flame, enkindle all the hearts in the whole country. Pass it from heart to heart. This will be the miracle. It will become a blaze that blinds Satan. I obtained the fire of love from the heavenly Father through the merits of my Son's wounds."

Hopefully, your love for Our Lady and her Son will increase as you read and pray this Spiritual Diary. (June 15, 1989)

Life of Elizabeth Szántò Kindelmann

(1913-1985)

Elizabeth Szántò was born in Budapest, a city of about 1.6 million people. Really, it is two cities, Buda and Pest, with the Danube River in the middle. She was the thirteenth child (preceded by six pairs of twins). She, alone, survived into adulthood.

Elizabeth never knew her mother. Her father died when she was about five. Because of her poor health, she lived for a time with her grandparents in the countryside. From ages 6 to 10, she attended elementary school. Then, she went to Switzerland, returned to Budapest, and later was supposed to be adopted by a Swiss family. However, she was late for the train and a young couple took her back to Budapest.

In Budapest began the struggle of a 13-year-old orphan who needed to find work so she did not starve. As a lonely orphan who was often taken advantage of, she had many different jobs. Twice she tried to enter religious congregations, but was rejected. Fortunately, she discovered a Father Motray who became her confessor for many years.

The turning point came in August 1929 when she was accepted for the parish choir. There she met Karoly Kindelmann, a chimneysweeper instructor (a good paying position). She was married at 16 (May 25, 1930). They had six children (1931 – 1942). In 1946, her husband died.

In 1948, the Communist Nationalization of Hungary was harsh. She was fired for political reasons (having a statue of the Blessed Mother in her home). By May 1951, she was in a humanly hopeless situation. Fortunately, she became a technical supervisor at a foundry (alluded to in the diary). This saved her family from starvation. She worked at a number of factories. Her children married and, with their grandchildren, moved back in with Elizabeth.

Her diary begins on July 13, 1960, when she wrote about the beginning religious experience that introduced her to God's presence. It speaks of three years of spiritual darkness (1958 - 1961) that prepared her for the locutions. The decisive moment came on July 16, 1961, the feast of Our Lady of Mount Carmel (Elizabeth was a lay Carmelite). This leads us into her diary, where she herself tells the story.

The History of Catholicism in Hungary

Christianity came early to Hungary, which was originally a Roman province. This is proven by the accounts of martyrdoms and the existence of Churches. In the late 10th century, the national leader, Beza, saw the need for Christianity for his people. So, he was baptized by St. Adalbert of Prague (986). His son, St. Stephen, was Hungary's first king. He organized the Church, establishing dioceses and Benedictine monasteries.

Hungary played a special role in world history as the bulwark of Western Christianity against the barbarians (11th and 12th centuries), and later against the Turks (15th century).

Calvinism entered Hungary in the 17th century and state-control of the Church began in the 18th century. A powerful secularism in the 19th century diluted many Catholic beliefs. With all of that, the church was sustained by many saints and Catholic movements. Catholic education was very strong. Most elementary schools were Catholic as well as a large number of high schools. Therefore, a strong Catholicism existed when Elizabeth was born in 1913.

By the treaty after World War I, 1920, Hungary lost 70% of its territory and 60% of its people. Its population became 7.5 million, of which 65% were Catholic. During Elizabeth's lifetime, Hungary lived under German occupation (1944), and then under Communism for the rest of her life.

During the 20th Century, Hungary had many martyrs and many heroes. Her diary does not at all allude to this political or social scene, with the exception of some locutions that speak to religious dispersed from their communities by Communism. She writes about her daily mass attendance, her meetings with the bishop and her spiritual directors. The picture is of normal parish life. Her diary begins in 1961. So, it was written under Communism, a proof that God's Spirit breathes wherever souls are open to Him.

Chapter One

Beginnings

God leads us on a road, which never ends, but we can turn away from him.

I was a widow with six children. All my cares destroyed my solitude and drew me away from God. After a long battle, my spiritual life died. I even asked why I had such a large family. I constantly lost my work and had to seek a new job. Even Satan would laugh at me, "If you did not have your children, you would have abandoned your struggle."

A great spiritual battle began within me. I still went to mass, but I felt empty. I deliberately went alone to the night mass so my children did not see me yawning, instead of praying.

The Turning Point

One day, I decided to stop going to mass. However, something happened. I did laundry all day Sunday until a few minutes before mass. Then, my child startled me, "Please hurry." However, at Church, I did not know how to speak with God. I thought about my Carmelite fast, "I will leave that all behind" (even though I kept it with no difficulty). When I returned home, I picked up my meditation book. However, my efforts to pray were in vain. A silence and coldness surrounded me. "God does not want to know me anymore."

Brother B's Funeral

I worked two shifts, early morning and afternoon. Within, I was greatly distressed. My inner thoughts blasphemed God. This battle lasted for three years. On June 15, 1961, I attended the burial of Brother B. I thought, "He has been a true Carmelite and has led a holy life." Inside, I heard his voice, "Do not cry. Return to Carmel."

The next day (Sunday, July 16, 1961), the feast of Our Lady of Mt. Carmel, I went to confession. I felt no sorrow, only a great dryness. I kept thinking of Brother B. His voice led me to the Blessed Virgin, "Go and prostrate before her." I did so but without feeling any peace. However, when I got home, I felt I had left my wounded soul at Carmel. In the silence of the night, I went into the garden, knelt before Our Lady of Lourdes and began to pray with fervor. The next day, I went to a little chapel where I often met Brother B. I prayed, "Heavenly Mother, my steps are so uncertain. Do not abandon me."

Continual Graces

During the following days, I received extraordinary graces. A man said, "I kneel next to you so I can be a saint, too." My eyes were always wet with tears and I tried to listen to God. After that, God spoke to me. How simple were these intimate conversations. Suddenly, I was overwhelmed by this devotion. Then, the demon said, "Do you think God can do this? If he had the power, he would." My heart sank and my mind went blank, until Jesus spoke, "Look at my disfigured face and my tortured body. Did I not suffer for souls? Believe in me and adore me." I made acts of faith and asked never to be separated from him. After this, I felt secure. Everything changed and I was drawn closer to him.

He kept urging me, "I want to give you greater graces. Renounce yourself."

"Jesus, am I capable of this?"

"Just will it and trust me," he answered.

My youngest son lived at home. Then, my married children with their families moved back in. At great sacrifice, I gave them my four-bedroom house with all the modern conveniences. As I gave them the house, I recalled the many memories of Christmas nights, weddings and baptisms. I remembered the poor food. Sometimes, we had only bread without butter, or vegetables without sauce. Even then, I made the table carefully so the children would not think that we were poor. The dining room, with all the memories, was difficult to give up. However, I moved into the children's bedroom and was filled with peace.

Total Sacrifice

Then, my youngest son got married. I gave them this bedroom and became totally poor. Jesus kept urging, "Renounce yourself completely." I wanted nothing to tie me to this world. So, I gave everything to the children. I felt I had done something foolish because I had nowhere to lay my head.

Everything seemed dark. What can I do with my life? The devil whispered, "You are not so old. Dress well. Enjoy yourself. If you have a chance, get married. You have completed your work as a mother."

Feeling abandoned, I asked Jesus, "Why have you left me alone?"

He answered, "For the good of your soul. Accept all that is still to come."

After this, I placed my daughter in charge, "From now on, you are the owner of this house. I will do whatever you want and eat whatever you give me."

She was surprised, "Mother, you are acting like a hermit."

No Job And No Home

My youngest daughter, whose husband was a professor, said, "I have to look for work. One salary is not enough." I gave up my good-paying job (painting plastics) so I could care for her two children. All of this happened in a few days. Jesus said, "Your will is free. I do not force you. Great riches lie in store for you."

On February 10, 1962, I had no home. This is what the Lord Jesus desired. On Sunday, the feast of Our Lady of Lourdes, I knelt in church, "Jesus, you have me here. I am completely detached from the world, just as you wanted."

Jesus answered, "You must live this way from now on, in the greatest humility."

After being in Church a long time, I wanted to go home. Jesus said, "Do not go yet." When I heard his voice, a river of repentance flooded my soul. The Blessed Virgin spoke, "Make reparation. He has been offended so often." I pondered these words and said, "Oh, Blessed Lady, if you are the one who asked me, direct my steps toward your Son."

Getting the Lord's House

The next day, I felt a strong impulse to get the key to the Church. The sister sacristan said she would ask the priest. Two days later, she gave me the key. To replace my house, the Lord was sharing his. How I loved this Church.

Being alone in the Church, I asked, "Jesus, are we alone?"

He answered, "Unfortunately, yes. Make great efforts so many will come."

Gratitude and sorrow filled my heart. "O Jesus, remove my faults by the blows of your chisel. I want to repent more than any repentant sinner." After I got the key, I visited him every night. It is impossible to describe those intimate hours.

Recording the Locutions

In the beginning of 1961, I did not record these conversations. After the Lord commanded me, I did write them down. I wrote short conversations, word for word. Often, his ideas went directly to my intellect without any words. One time, He asked me to pray on Monday night for priests in purgatory. On another occasion, I asked to experience his infinite goodness. He said, "Do not ask for yourself but for those for whom you pray." I asked pardon for being selfish.

Chapter Two

1962

The Beginnings

In the first week of March, I did not know what was happening. Every five minutes, the Lord urged me to kneel down to make reparation. I asked to share in his work to the greatest possible degree. He said, "Ask for abundant graces. The more you ask, the more you will receive. Many ask to share in my work but when I ask for a sacrifice, they grow frightened." Jesus kept saying that I had to live for him every moment, without interruption. He often complained about consecrated souls, "They live more for the world than for my redemptive work." He said, "Do not spare yourself. Know no limit. Do not separate yourself from my work for even one moment."

The Lord asked me to contact a religious sister. When I spoke about the state of my soul and my great darkness she said, "This might be autosuggestion." This greatly upset me and I thought that all of my experiences were an illusion. That night, I said, "Lord, what is going on with me? Where have I allowed myself to be led? What is true?" Only someone who has suffered this temptation can understand. The next day, at Holy Communion, I recovered my peace.

Fast For Priests

Jesus said, "I ask something great from you. Every Thursday and Friday, fast on bread and water and offer this fast for 12 special priests (Hungarian priests who will be entrusted with this devotion). On both days, spend four hours in my Divine Presence to make reparation. On Fridays, from noon to three, adore my Sacred Body and Precious Blood. Keep the Friday fast until 3:00 PM, the hour my Body was lowered from the cross. Accepting this sacrifice will gain extraordinary graces.

"Commit yourself to this fast for twelve weeks so the twelve priests will be ready to carry out my plans. You will know who should take my petition to these twelve priests. They, too, must make reparation and be immersed in my Sacred Passion. These twelve priests are the best in the country."

Future Trials

Jesus also spoke about future trials, "You will suffer a great spiritual dryness. Different temptations will torment you. Have total confidence. This is the key to my heart." He added, "In temptations, flee to our Mother. She will defend you from the Evil One." Since I was so forceful, Jesus said, "You are intense, forceful and irritable. You must be transformed according to my heart. Do not be upset that you can only make small sacrifices."

Jesus the Teacher

On April 8, Jesus said, "I want you entirely for myself. Nothing, not even a hair, must separate you and I." I responded, "Lord, I am only a beginner." He reminded me about my schooling. "A few months ago, you wanted to register in high school. I opposed this because I wanted you in my school. Now you rejoice and are a happy student. I am the teacher, dedicated to you from morning until night."

I answered, "Lord, the problem is that I understand very little."

"That is true," he replied.

Later, Jesus said, "Draw close to my Mother."

I replied, "She is the one who invited me to adore. I was confused until I heard her voice."

He said, "That first meeting (July 1961) was the great step. My Mother entrusted you to me in a special way. After that, you flew to me like an arrow and never looked back at earth. Since your birth, I have awaited you."

I said, "Lord, never let go of me." "I did not let go of you, you let go of me." Jesus lamented, "When you were a widow, you asked your children for help. How sad when they excused themselves. How many children I have. If only they would help for one hour."

The Divine Choice

After receiving these great graces, I exclaimed, "God, what have you done with me? Why do I no longer value earth? I cannot understand. Why me? Are there not pure souls who are worthy of you."

Jesus said, "From among the worst sinners, I choose souls for my work. If they accept, I fill them with great graces." Then he said, "Use all your strength to bring sinners to me. Give no thought to anything else. By your desires you have entered entirely into my heart."

To prepare me, Jesus said, "A great battle awaits you, but you will conquer in the sign of the cross. When you make the cross, think of the three Divine Persons. Make the sign of the cross five times, while thinking of my Five Wounds. Always look at my eyes bathed in blood. Tell everyone all that I tell you. Do not worry about how to make the Cause prevail. Be a good Carmelite. Be humble and refrain your tongue, not saying unneeded words. Do not worry that you can only give me little things."

Ordering the Week

One day, the Lord said, "On Monday, pray for the Holy Souls, offering a strict fast and prayer during the night. Each time you fast, you will free a priest's soul from purgatory. Whoever practices this fast will themselves be freed within eight days after their death.

"On Tuesday, pray for the family and make spiritual communions for each member. My Mother will take each under her protection. Offer night prayer for them. Invoke St. Joseph every day. He will help you.

"On Wednesday, pray for priestly vocations. Many young men have these desires, but they do not meet anyone to help them to gain the goal. Your night vigil will gain abundant graces.

"On Thursday, make reparation to the Blessed Sacrament. Offer the strict fast and night prayer for the twelve priests.

"On Friday, immerse yourself in my Sacred Passion. During the day, meditate on the Way of the Cross. From noon to three, adore my sacred wounds." (Note, this can be done even at work or school.)

"On Saturday, venerate my Mother in a special way. Seek the grace of a holy death for priests in their final agony. Priest souls in heaven will intercede for you."

Concerning Sunday, the Redeemer gave no specific instructions.

First Message From Our Lady

On April 13, Good Friday, I asked the Blessed Virgin to engrave His wounds into my heart. My tears flowed. She herself was sobbing. "There is so much sin in this country (Hungary). Help me. Let us save this country. I will place a beam of light in your hands. This is the Flame of Love of my heart. Add your love to the Flame of Love and pass it to others."

I asked, "Mother, why do you not work miracles like you did at Fatima, so people will believe in you?"

She replied, "The more miracles I work, the fewer who believe. I asked for the First Saturdays and no one paid attention.

"King Saint Stephen consecrated your country to me. (St. Stephen was the first King of Hungary, in 1000 A.D.) I promised him that I would gather his intercession and that of all the Hungarian saints into my heart.

"I place this new instrument in your hands. Accept it with great understanding because I gaze on Hungary with great sorrow. The twelve priests will be the most worthy to fulfill my request. Take this flame. You are the first to whom I entrust it. It is the Flame of Love of my Heart. First, light your own heart and then, pass it on to others."

She sobbed so much I could hardly hear her. In the name of Hungary, I promised her everything to relieve her sorrow.

Family Holy Hour

Mary added another request. "On Thursday and Friday there must be a family holy hour. When two or three are together, my Son is present. Begin by making the sign of the cross five times. Do the same at the conclusion. Do this also when rising, going to bed and during the day. This draws your heart to the Eternal Father.

Miracle of the Flame

Mary explained, "With this flame you will light all the hearts in the world. The miracle will be this. This flame will become a fire, and with its shining light, this fire will blind Satan."

I made excuses, "I am not worthy" and "How can I accomplish this?"

Mary said, "I will be with you and I will take you into my heart." She added, "Take my Son's petition to Father E."

The Role of Carmel

On April 15, Mary said, "Let the Carmelite Fathers be the first to receive the Flame of Love and spread it. My flame will go forth from Carmel, because they are the ones most called to honor me. Take two little candles. Light your candle first, and then the other. After this, give it to my Son. He will spread the Flame among my twelve chosen priests. They will not be all Carmelite priests.

"After these priests have come together, let this devotion begin in twelve churches dedicated to me. In this ceremony, they will pass the lighted candle from one to another. Let each person take the candle home and begin family prayer in the same way."

Two days later, Jesus said, "Ask my priests to speak of my beloved Mother. They should never give a homily without exhorting people to deep devotion to her." He also reminded me of my task, "Desire many souls for me. This is your life's purpose and you must always keep this before your eyes."

Homesick for Heaven

In April, I wondered at how I could accomplish everything. Jesus spoke in my soul. "Just do my redeeming work unceasingly. Do not ask how. Just be anxious that my Kingdom arrives for you and others."

The next day, a sharp burning pain burdened my heart. Although I suffered, the pain pleased me. I didn't know what to compare it with. Jesus explained that this was homesickness for heaven. "As a child you were far from your mother and your country. This strong sorrow that I send you is a longing for your heavenly home."

Today, Jesus said, "Quickly pass on my Mother's Flame of Love so that my heavenly Father's chastising hand departs from Hungary. Do not delay any more. The great woman of Hungary (Our Lady) will confirm your work."

During these days, I felt a strong attraction to bring these messages to a priest, Father E. I went to the Lord. He told me not to delay. I was fearful, knowing that there was no more time for a delay.

Saying "Goodbye"

Then, the Evil One oppressed me and I lay prostrate before Jesus' feet. An indescribable love came into my trembling soul and an extraordinary sensation traveled all through my body and soul. Then, Jesus spoke in great sorrow, "This is the night to say 'Good bye.' Until now, you have heard my pleasant words. Now, I will cover you in silence. I will deprive you of hearing my words and of sensing my presence. The Evil One breathed a sigh of relief and said, "My hour has come." The Lord said, "I must do this for the good of your soul."

The Holy Spirit breathed upon me a different level of his powers so I could overcome all temptations. Jesus said, "Do not misunderstand. I will continue to be with you in Holy Communion as I was today." These were Jesus' parting words and they left me sorrowful. Previously, Jesus awakened me for the night prayer. Now my Guardian Angel awakened me. Oh what a difference!

Delivering the Message

On April 27, I went to Father E and said, "I have a letter for you." Inside was our Lord's message. I waited until he finished. He looked surprised, "I cannot reply to this."

I said, "I wasn't looking for a reply. I have already suffered much for the Cause." I left with a downcast spirit. I went to church and complained to the Blessed Mother, "Whom did you send me to? He rejected me and did not say a helpful word." However, the priest did tell me to see Father X.

A few days later, I found Father X's confessional and explained my condition. Although I had never met him, I opened my soul completely. I asked him to direct me and to tell me if I am in error. He found nothing out of order. So, I returned home very calm. The next time, I was to bring him the written messages and he would discuss them with the other priests.

Clear Directions

On April 30, Our Lady was very clear. "Entrust these messages to the priests with responsibility. Tell them not to fear. There will be twelve Churches, four Churches in Budapest that are dedicated to me and eight other churches with the best attendance. Begin the devotion of the Flame of Love in all twelve churches at the same time."

On May 2, I took these messages to Father X, only to discover that he was in the hospital with a serious operation. The Flame of Love had suffered a new setback. Jesus spoke, "Do not fear. My Sacred Heart will be your permanent refuge. My eyes watch over those who work for me and my heart suffers for those who do not." His heart was so sad and I felt such anguish that all my physical strength was weakened.

The Country's Beggar

A few days later, Jesus said, "I am this country's beggar. Even though begging is forbidden, yet I keep begging. I go from street to street, from house to house and from village to village.

"My hand is always extended but I receive only a small donation. People quickly close the door of their heart. I hardly get to see inside and I am forced to leave quickly. My graces accumulate in my heart. To make up for others, you must seek many graces. I am in debt to you.

"I have called many souls to follow me on the road of reparation, but few understand. You must sacrifice so that their numbers will increase. These souls will counterbalance my just anger. My Mother keeps back my wrath. Her Flame of Love obliges even me."

Beginning Mystical Experiences

On May 2, the sister assigned to me asked, "What difference did you experience when your Guardian Angel woke you up instead of the Lord?" I could not answer. My Lord no longer speaks to me and prayer has become a monologue.

While kneeling before the Lord, a great brightness shone before my spiritual eyes. It was like a living light sending out particles of light in every direction. I could not find words to express it. It gave me the sensation that I was a creature privileged to deal with its Creator.

On Tuesdays, I make Spiritual Communions for my children. However, deprived of Jesus' words and presence, I was dried up by a great spiritual thirst. Jesus spoke, "One Our Father or one Hail Mary said in spiritual dryness is more fruitful than prayers said in spiritual fervor." A great calm descended. Then I experienced a great power as the people in church chanted the Litany of the Blessed Virgin.

Made Ready

On May 4, Our Blessed Mother spoke, "You are over this great temptation. I will reward you. We wanted to increase your humility. My Son let Satan get so near to you, to make you ready to pass on the Flame of Love. Make sacrifices for the twelve priests. They, too, will suffer.

"You must spread my Cause. Do not be afraid. The Flame is gentle and will arouse no suspicions. The miracle will come forth in your hearts. On Candlemas (February 2), my chosen workers will hand each other a candle. In this way, the Flame of Love will be a living fire in their hearts. Prepare everything so that it will spread like wildfire."

I said, "Jesus promised me that you would guide me."

Then, she replied, "Go to my beloved priest, Father X. He will do everything as I would. He will be my messenger to the Churches. He will not be opposed to the Cause nor will he excuse himself." Between May 3rd and 11th, the Blessed Virgin told me four times not to neglect her command.

Asking Her for Sacrifices

After Jesus complained, I said, "How many times, Jesus, I have written down your sad complaints, but I can do very little."

He replied, "The burning of your heart can lessen the burning sorrow of my heart. When the number who help my redemptive work is great, I will not complain. From you, I need a greater acceptance of sacrifices. Renounce the reading of frivolous books, the hearing of your favorite music and your seeking to be among others. I want you to increase your fasts. Do not give yourself to any pleasure. Let your breakfast and your afternoon snack be bread and water. At your principal meal you can have other foods, but make them tasteless. Eat only to nourish your body.

The Night Vigil

"You must give up more of your sleep. Rise twice each night, for one hour. Can I count on you? I, the God-Man, ask this of you."

I said, "My soul is ready but my body is weak. A war goes on within me. Sweet Jesus, I am yours. Dispose of me as you wish."

The night vigil was very difficult. To rise from sleep cost me much. I asked the Blessed Virgin, "My Mother, wake me up. When my Guardian Angel wakes me, it is not effective."

The next night, the Blessed Virgin woke me up. I spoke to her while lying in bed. She said, "Stay in bed. A mother can speak with her daughter any place and any time. I prayed at night because Joseph worked hard during the day. On Sunday, your day of rest, assist at as many masses as possible. You must never rest. My Son asks you to continually share in his redeeming work."

The Great Prayer

My Redeemer asked me to say this prayer, which expresses his longings:

> May our feet journey together.
>
> May our hands gather in unity.
>
> May our hearts beat in unison.
>
> May our souls be in harmony.
>
> May our thoughts be as one.
>
> May our ears listen to the silence together.
>
> May our glances profoundly penetrate each other.
>
> May our lips pray together to gain mercy from the Eternal Father.

I made this prayer completely my own. Jesus said, "Through this prayer, Satan will be blind and souls will not be led into sin."

Satan's Wild Anger

On May 14, the Blessed Virgin woke me up. "Satan is destroying souls at a mind-boggling pace. I need your efforts. Sorrow consumes my soul because I see how many souls are condemned."

Three days later, Mary said, "The wild anger of Satan increases. He wants to dominate even persevering souls. Help me." Sorrow filled my heart and I had to stop writing due to my tears.

I asked, "Mother, what can I do?"

She answered, "Go, speak with my children. They will be my delegates."

I protested, "You must speak. I am a nobody. They pay no attention to me even though I bring your words. I am being destroyed because the priest you sent me to does not accept your request."

Later, Jesus warned me, "The Evil One wants to enter and destroy the powers of your soul like a ravaging animal."

"Jesus, how can this be? As soon as I awake, I give myself to you." He answered, "You must do this all day, not just when you awake."

The Dream

On May 23, the beating of Jesus' heart resonated in my heart with a sweetness that I had never experienced. He continued to give me this gift. The following is a dream, which I did not write down for a week. Today, Jesus told me to record it.

> I saw strange-looking men next to a large black disc. I felt that they were the worst devils. They were putting a sheet of iron over the disk to hide it. When finished, they expressed their

satisfaction.

On the right, there were white clouds. I saw a good person, accompanied by three others. They were enemies of the Evil One and plotted how to destroy the disk. The Evil One, with great sarcasm, said to them, "You can look at it. We have made it well and it will cause you many headaches." I saw a small opening and knew that we could succeed in removing the cover. I decided to tell those on the right.

Then, I woke up. I could not understand the dream but I believed that we could make the disk transparent again if we worked hard.

Taking Away the Dryness

In May, Jesus spoke to me again, after a long absence. As I went shopping, he drew near and said, "I do not bother you, do I?" I could not contain my tears and I said those words, which he loved to hear, "With insatiable thirst, I desire you."

As he spoke, the spiritual dryness was gone. I know this consolation was for the good of my soul. He continued, "Always be silent so God's voice can speak within you. In silence, your spiritual life sends out roots. Each morning, offer your sacrifices and you will receive the flames of my love. During the day, do not let the flame of sacrifice go out." Then, he promised, "I would speak to every soul this way, if they would receive me."

Interpreting the Dream

In the morning, Jesus interpreted the dream. "The black disk is your country. The white cloud is my Mother and the person next to her is my beloved priest who is ready to do everything." He never said who this priest was and I did not ask him. Jesus explained, "The disk's blackness signifies the seven capital sins.

The iron seems to be one but it is really seven sheets. The top sheet is lust. It is thin and resistant, and must be bent by prayer and sacrifice to be removed.

"The second sheet is negligence in doing good. Made of unbreakable metal, it cannot be bent. It must be broken into small particles by great effort. I will be with you in this work. Only unceasing labor can remove negligence in doing good because the disk is hard."

Our Lady pleaded, "Do not delay. Everyone has already wasted too much time. The Evil One works with greater success than everyone. Elizabeth, do not fear the devil who always encircles you. I have crushed him. Hide beneath my mantle and frequently kiss the scapular that you wear."

The Baptismal Suit

Jesus explained many truths, "When a father buys his son a new suit, he wants the son to be careful with the suit. At Baptism, my heavenly Father gave everyone the beautiful suit of sanctifying grace, but they do not take care of it.

"I instituted the sacrament of confession, but they do not use it. I suffered indescribable torments on the cross and hid myself within a host like a child wrapped in swaddling clothes. They must be careful when I enter their hearts that I do not find clothing that is torn and dirty.

"People say prayers without feeling or attention. This happens day after day, year after year. They should speak to me in simple words. You, Elizabeth, do not leave me alone. Draw souls close to me whenever you can."

Using the Sacrament of Penance

On May 24, Jesus said, "Kiss these hands for those to whom I have extended them in vain."

I asked, "Do you extend your hands to some who pay no attention?"

He responded, "Yes, and I will have to raise a severe hand against them as their Judge. I have filled some souls with precious treasures. If they used the Sacrament of Penance to polish these treasures, they would shine again. But they have no interest and are distracted by the world's glitter."

I cannot record all of the Lord's words because some went directly to my consciousness. When I had to leave, he asked, "Will we continue to be united?" I said, "We are never separated. We cannot live without each other." We both said these words together. I don't know who said them first.

New Consolations

On June 2, at Church, I took out my prayer book. Jesus said, "Put away your book and we will pray." Great emotion overwhelmed me. I turned to the Blessed Virgin, "I can hardly stand his overwhelming graces. I cannot even pronounce the words."

She said, "Respond with sorrow for your sins." A deep repentance filled my soul. At Holy Communion, he filled my soul and took away several days of spiritual dryness.

The Savior woke me up for night prayer and said, "In the quiet of the night, I seek souls." I was so touched by his tenderness, that he said, "Since this pleases you, I will always awaken you with these words, 'In the quiet of the night, I seek souls.'"

At the end of my two hours of prayer, Jesus said, "Suffer with me. Feel with me! Relieve my sorrow." My spiritual eyes saw a vision that broke my heart and for a few minutes, I was suffocating.

The Lord's Sorrow

On July 12, the Lord complained, "You see that almost no one is doing anything. The Flame of Love is not making progress. You must stir up the fire because you have been chosen."

I said, "Jesus, you know the burning desire of my heart and how I suffer because nothing has been done."

Three days later, the Lord was again filled with sorrow. "Since when did devout souls start making me wait? My patience has no limit. I promise to draw them to me but they are not attracted to me."

I had fasted for nine days. As I ate, Jesus said, "Invite me as a guest to your little breakfast table and bring me your frailties." "O Jesus, I want to repent of my sins as no one has ever repented before." Jesus responded, "I place a single drop of my blood upon your sorrow. I pardon your sins fully and I forget them."

Elizabeth's Sorrow for Father X

The next day, I was burdened with sorrow over Father X and his illness. Our Lady spoke, "Offer your sorrow for his healing."

"Will he be healed?" I asked.

"Yes, in a short while, but not for a long time. He will come to me because he is already on the road. He is my beloved Son whom I hold deeply in my heart."

On July 20, Jesus said, "At your meals, stop eating what is tasty. Only in this way, will I be your guest. What is tasty for you is tasteless for me."

The Virgin asked me to place the parish community under her patronage and that of St. Joseph. Every day, I must ask for the grace of a happy death for souls.

Feast of Corpus Christi

For weeks, I meditated exclusively on Jesus' Sacred Body and Precious Blood. The experiences were indescribable. The Evil One said, "I could do greater miracles." I replied, "Only if God permitted and you cannot save anyone." My words completely disarmed him and he stopped bothering me.

On July 30, Jesus complained about indifferent souls. "My love receives no response from them." The sorrow of Jesus' heart breaks my heart open. When this happens, I stop writing.

Mary urged me, "Intensify your desires so that my Flame of Love is put into action." In response, I ate only bread and water with a little fruit for nine days. She asked a second time. So, I deprived myself of water. Due to the heat, this was difficult but my heart always feels extraordinary strength.

Blinding Satan

On August 1, the Lord woke me up at 3:00 AM. "I seek hearts in the loneliness of the night." After he left, I decided to pray that the Flame of Love would be ignited. The devil filled me with anguish, but when I was immersed in the Flame of Love, the anguish disappeared and my soul felt light. It was like my body had been moved away, and only my soul was left.

Then, I was knocked to my knees, and it seemed that my soul was covered with beggar's clothing. The Blessed Virgin covered me with the scapular and said, "Many souls in Hungary are dressed in rags. With your help, I will cover them with my mantle." She allowed me to experience the effects of the grace of her Flame of love, for myself and for all of Hungary.

She said, "Satan has been blinded for some hours, now. He has lost power. It is especially the sin of lust that covers so many victims. The evil spirits are frightened and inactive. They do not understand what has happened. Satan has stopped giving them orders. Souls are free from his power. Tomorrow, when they awaken, millions will seek a conversion." She allowed me to see what these souls are experiencing.

At Church, the next morning, she said, "The inextinguishable fire of my Flame of Love is burning in your soul. You see how wonderful it is. I have never given you such a powerful force of grace. Since the Word became Flesh, I have never given such a great movement as the Flame of Love that comes to you now. Until now, there has been nothing that so blinds Satan. Do not refuse this gift. To do so, would bring great ruin.

In Carmel

"My Flame of Love will be lit first in Carmel. They are called to venerate me the most. Also, the Daughters of the Holy Spirit must collaborate in spreading the Flame of Love. The Flame will be lit and will reach the whole world, not just in nations that have been faithful. I will aid your work with miracles never seen before. This will bring about reparation to my Son." She continued, "I ask the Holy Father to make the Feast of the Flame of Love on February 2, Candlemas day. I do not want a special feast."

A Family Feud

On August 3, I went for adoration from noon to 3:00 PM. However, I was distressed by a family disagreement that keeps getting repeated. Jesus spoke, "I see your great efforts. They are not in vain. I will free your family from the Evil One who disturbs their peace. Trust me."

"They will need a miracle," I said.

"Cannot I work a miracle?" He replied. "I will so bless this impossible problem that it will be straightened out. I cannot deny my Mother anything when she uses her Flame of Love."

Putting Out Satan's Fire

On August 6, Jesus complained, "No soul entrusted to my priests should be condemned. The word, condemnation causes me sorrow. I would suffer death again, even a thousand times, because a condemned soul has no hope. Unite your desire for souls with my Precious Blood. This will be a miraculous instrument."

I felt Jesus' sorrow. It was so sharp that I almost collapsed. "O Jesus, I will make every effort so no soul is condemned."

A day later, Jesus continued, "If a fire begins, do not people put it out? Why do you not put out Satan's fire? How many look on in cowardice. They will be responsible. They close their eyes and let souls be condemned. Oh, consecrated souls do not be lazy. Laziness is the root of every evil in your soul. It leads to despair and you are unaware of its presence."

Jesus then spoke of my martyrdom, "Your inner martyrdom is my will and Satan cannot stop it. This inner battle brings forth great fruit, just as external martyrdom does. You must never be half hearted."

The Family

On August 8, Jesus spoke of the early years of my marriage, of the family night prayer and of the ejaculatory prayers, "With your longings, you desired many souls. I listened to you. Many souls were converted and came to know me. I value your desires. I had an uninterrupted desire to save souls. Let this same desire burn in your heart."

Our Lady also spoke, "Hungarian families are torn apart. With my Flame of Love I want the home to come alive again with love. I want to unite scattered families. Help me! My flame of Love being lit depends on you."

Gathering An Army

During August, Jesus said, "All are invited to join my special fighting force. The coming of my Kingdom must be your only purpose in life. My words will reach a multitude of souls. Trust! I will help all of you in a miraculous way." He continued, "Do not love comfort. Do not be cowards. Do not wait. Confront the storm to save souls. Give yourselves to the work. If you do nothing, you abandon the earth to Satan and to sin. Open your eyes and see all the dangers that claim victims and threaten your own souls."

He asked me to bring all his words to those in authority, "They must not discard my request. Let them embrace my desire and begin a new life." Jesus spoke to the priests involved, "You priests preach about the Cause but you do not act. Great efforts are needed for my Kingdom to come. Do not live as hypocrites."

Success of the Cause

On August 16, He complained again, "Many consecrated souls live a carefree life, wasting their time in idleness and seeking their own desires. They throw me little scraps, as if I am a beggar. To you, consecrated souls, I will have to say, 'Depart from me. You have not fulfilled what I wanted you to do.'"

Our Lady promised, "In spite of objections, bad intentions and obstacles, my Cause will succeed. Always be humble. Only a humble soul can fulfill our Cause." Jesus added," No one can destroy God's plan. However, my redeeming work needs everyone's cooperation. I do not want to lose any of you. Satan takes up his battle against the human race as never before.

A Cheerful Spirit

Jesus instructed me, "Always be joyful. Do not let anyone disturb your cheerful spirit. Be careful of your Baptismal wedding garment. Let all know that you will share in the heavenly banquet. Desire that everyone have this same yearning. Let the coming of my kingdom be your only purpose in life. Be valiant and testify to me before all."

I told the Lord that I would like to have a spiritual director. He answered, "Why are you impatient? It is my responsibility to get you a director. Do not fear. I will give you a director according to my own heart. I will never abandon you." His words gave great peace.

Consecrate Your Homes to the Sacred Heart

Because of all my efforts at nightly prayer, the Lord promised that He himself would wake me up. I am happy when He awakens me. The night prayer goes quickly. I want to record a special happening. One summer night, as we finished our conversation, he paused for a long time in front of our house. He spoke of the virtues practiced by my children when they were small and of the merits of our family prayer.

He appreciated that our family was consecrated to the Sacred Heart and practiced that devotion. Suddenly, he said, "I bless this house that is consecrated to my Sacred Heart." This blessing was a sublime experience. He said, "My Mother obliges me to bless your family because, with every longing of your heart, you desire to spread her Flame of Love."

The Value of Silence

All seems dark and insecure. The difficulties that prevent the Cause from moving forward, came against me. I cried out to Jesus and Mary, "Without you, I am nothing. Hold me, tightly."

Once, as I wanted to leave after morning mass to work in the garden in the good weather, Jesus said, "Do not go. Why are you in such a hurry? I called you close to me. Do you prefer something else? Do you not trust the value of your sufferings? Your sufferings have great value."

On another occasion, he said, "Be quiet. Do you know who is truly wise? The one who is silent. I prepared by thirty years of silence for just three years of activity. Speak only when I give you the signal. Speak only what I taught you. Few words will produce abundant fruit."

Silence reigned in my soul. He filled my soul with his divine presence. This caused me to tremble. Until now, nothing has been this intense. My body was wiped out and my soul was filled with divine grace.

Experiences

On August 21, the Lord spoke in a new tone of voice. "Draw close to me without fear. When I give you my brightness, you will never notice the darkness of your own soul. For me, time does not exist. I call some souls quickly to Myself. You fly like an arrow to heaven and do not turn back to earth."

On August 25, I saw the face of a priest in a spiritual vision. However, I did not know him. A few days later, my daughter showed me a photo of Father Biro, a Jesuit priest whom I had never met. He was a great soul. Next to his photo were his famous words, "Even if I have to suffer until I die, I have lost nothing if I become a saint." Something exploded in my soul and the difficulties caused by the Evil One were removed. (Note: Father Biro, S.J., 1869–1938, founded a Catholic Publishing House and the Sacred Heart Sisters in Budapest.)

Three days later, Jesus directed me, "Do nothing from your own will. Bring everything to your spiritual director. Leave the rest to him. His words will always come from me."

Parish Representative

On one occasion, Jesus said, "From now on you will pray in the name of the parish community. You will pray in the name of all, even of those who are not interested. I have chosen you to be the intercessor for Budapest. This is a priestly dignity. Do not forget the sick. Take care that not one soul is condemned.

"You always wanted to go to the missions. That was impossible. You had to mature in the womb of your family. Your principal missionary work will always be your family. The work there is not finished. Be interested principally in priestly vocations." Jesus continued his long conversation, "Never be content with yourself. There is no room for self-satisfaction. Work as hard as possible. Do not think about rest. You will be abundantly rewarded for your tiredness."

The Blessed Virgin promised, "You must take my Flame of Love to the other side of the ocean." I do not know how I will fulfill this. Our Lady did not explain. (Note: The movement arrived in Ecuador, went to Mexico and is now in Canada and the United States.)

Battles With Satan

When I went to Church for the three hours of adoration, the devil tried to flatter me by saying that I am unique and no human being can live this life. God wants a normal life for me, not the foolish way I dress and eat or take enjoyments. As I meditated upon Jesus' sufferings, he shouted in rage, "I will wait no longer." When he comes at me, I give myself to Jesus and Mary. They use me to blind him.

These battles exhaust me, but when I realize that I suffer for the Flame of Love, all becomes easy. The greatest suffering is total darkness accompanied by doubts. When these invade me, I can hardly walk.

The next day, as I was kneeling at the altar, the Evil One's terrifying presence shook me. The devil spoke, "Do you know that this is pure imagination? You are trying to get attention. You are incapable of doing great things."

I began to think, "I do not want to sin. How have I gotten involved in this terrible sin?" I knelt at the altar, "Jesus, I am very fearful." My confused thoughts began to calm down. Jesus spoke, "Do not fear. I will not allow anyone to harm you."

These words caused an inner illumination and I recalled Our Lady's words a few days ago, "Let us set out with St. Joseph. You must walk with us along Bethlehem's dark roads. We must seek lodging for my Flame of Love, which is Jesus Christ himself." After her words, my strength of soul carried me. We traveled those dark roads and looked for lodging but everyone rejected us.

In early September, I enjoyed an extraordinary mental state and Jesus spoke every day. "I need you for my saving work and I ask total giving." I said, "O Jesus, can I do anything else? I live for you and I die for you. Divine Sculptor, form me in your own image. Just recognize your work at the hour of my death."

Bring to the Pope

On September 3, Our Lady said, "Soon, the first official step will be taken. This should have already happened. Tell our spiritual director of my desire. He must bring the Cause to the Primate Bishop of Hungary and then to the Roman Pontiff, Vicar of my Son on Earth. There has never been a time of grace like this since the Word became Flesh. Blinding Satan will shake the world."

Mary's Promise

A few days later, Our Lady gave a great promise, "From now on, when any of you are at prayer during the night vigil, I will give you the grace so that the Flame of Love blesses dying persons in the whole world. I will blind Satan so this Flame will save the dying from eternal damnation."

I was filled with joy but then I doubted. Did I correctly understand? How can I receive this immense grace? Did the Blessed Virgin really say something? I do not understand. The Evil One has me so confused.

Great Doubts

When I say the rosary, I just repeat, "O miraculous Virgin, I believe in you." My lips say this but my mind refuses to accept it. I pleaded, "O Blessed Virgin, dispel my doubts. Is it possible and permissible to believe this?" The Blessed Virgin gave no reply, so I asked the Lord. He said, "You get this answer only from my Mother." I asked, "Lord, will you abandon me?" He said, "Accept this miraculous power not just with your lips but also with your mind." I tried that but my mind refused to accept it. "O Jesus, if I refuse to accept, will I sin against the Virgin Mary? I have no spiritual director to help me through." I kept repeating for hours, "O miraculous Virgin, I believe in you."

The Great Relief

I went to the religious sister and told her the Blessed Virgin's message. She accepted everything with simple faith. A smile came across her lips and her faith dispelled my doubts. She turned to the statue of the Blessed Virgin, "O holy Virgin, you are all powerful." In admiration of the Flame of Love, we prayed for the greatest number of souls to be saved from eternal damnation. She gave me a lot of advice. She did not know the great peace that Jesus gave me through her.

Walking the Road to Bethlehem

On September 15, the Blessed Virgin said that many souls are lost due to a superficial lack of understanding. She does all she can, but consecrated souls refuse everything. Then she added, "Because of your humility, my Flame of Love will move gently ahead, without any force. Be careful. Stay hidden. You will live in continual humiliations. This way, I can guard you and give you the Flame of Love.

Come with me. We will walk the roads of Bethlehem. There will be just the three of us—St. Joseph, you, and me." The Blessed Virgin allows me to experience her sorrow. Some days, I can hardly walk. My eyes are filled with tears and I try to avoid everyone. I want only to fulfill all she wants.

Satan increases my sufferings. He says, "In every way, you are useless. Why do they not entrust these matters to the bishop? An intelligent person would not even talk with you. Even the priests, to whom they have sent you, do not accept your message. Be sensible. It is useless."

Once, as I was leaving Church, Jesus asked, "Why are you leaving so quickly? Is there anything so important as I? Just tell me that you love and adore me. Our thoughts must be one—to save souls from eternal damnation. Do you know how much my soul suffers because souls are lost?"

Fast for Priests

On September 28, Jesus said, "How will I reward you? From now on, if a person fasts for a deceased priest, by that fast the priest's soul will be freed from purgatory, eight days after his death. Anyone who observes this fast, will free a suffering soul."

My soul rejoiced when I heard of this new grace. "Jesus, I want your grace to be known publicly." He repeated his promise, "By observing this fast, priests will be freed from purgatory on the eighth day after their death."

Thursdays and Fridays

The Flame of Love continually fills my soul. At Church, our Lady spoke, "You must see Thursday and Friday as days of great grace. During the hours of reparation, the power of Satan will weaken to the degree that you pray for sinners. I have given to you the task of making known this love. Never believe you are important. Consider yourself as nothing. Always do this."

The Blessed Virgin commanded me to write her words in a detailed form for those who will spread her Flame of Love.

A Visit to Father X

I went to the hospital to visit Father X. When I was alone, I asked Father if he remembered me. He recognized me only after I spoke of the Cause. I asked him to read about the Flame of Love. He said, "I cannot even read my breviary or the mail."

Then, he looked at me with his eyes half-opened and with a light that was not of this world. He was contemplating God. "I am a victim. I gave myself over fully to Jesus and Mary. I choose nothing. They do with me as they see best."

I told him what Our Lady said, "I will restore him quickly but not for long." I asked, "Father, what will I do with the Flame of Love?"

He responded, "I can do nothing. Have confidence. The Blessed Virgin can arrange everything." I almost collapsed from these months of spiritual suffering. "Father, I, too, undergo sufferings. I am like the living dead." The nurse came and ended the visit. I kissed his hand because I might not see him again.

As I went immediately to Church, great darkness weighed upon me. I said, "Jesus, I have come here to complain. I am sinful and you trust me with this matter for the whole world. I am weak and useless. Please entrust this to a worthy soul."

The Lord's Directions

On October 1, Jesus said, "You know what I told you. We must go up to Calvary. I permit you to feel alone so you gain merits. Do not be upset about not having a spiritual director. I am directing you. Sometimes, I will send other persons to help. Accept that person even if they seem insignificant."

For two days, Jesus has been saying that I must try again to put into action the Flame of Love. I must go back to those who rejected me. I was shaken by his words. The previous embarrassment and rigid refusal penetrated me like a sharp sorrow. I thought, "'Is this really the Lord Jesus who speaks in my soul?" As I was going back and forth, Jesus said, "You must humble yourself in every way."

The next day, Mary said, "Remember what I told you about setting out on the dark road to Bethlehem? Come with St. Joseph and me. The Flame of Love seeks lodging. Get close to St. Joseph. He will accompany you."

The Lord Speaks

While I knelt before the Blessed Sacrament, Jesus said, "You are very distracted today and have hardly lifted your heart to me. I long for your words." As I looked at the host, it seemed that the monstrance turned slightly toward me.

Jesus rebuked me, "You have wasted the seeds of your word on trifles. Your seeds only mature in the Divine Sun. We need each drop of oil that can be squeezed from every seed."

On October 5, Jesus said, "My heart suffers because of consecrated souls. I walk with them but they do not recognize me. They live in wasteful laziness, seeking only their own comfort. They act as if they were not my workers.

"O tepid souls, do not force me to raise my sacred hands to curse you. Was my Sacred Body crucified in vain? Do you not see what I have done for you? Is not your heart moved? Do you not want to share in my sufferings? Why are you standing here doing nothing? I suffered for you but you excuse yourselves. Be crucified as I was crucified. This is the only way to have eternal life."

Jesus said to me, "Always ask. I am happy to distribute my treasures. You will cash them in at your death. Human words cannot express what I have prepared for you in heaven. At your arrival, my heart will skip a beat. Those whom you freed from purgatory will welcome you. Like good friends, they will await you. This joy will never end.

Mary spoke, "I will await you in heaven. Our drops of oil will fall upon earth, on those lamps, which are flickering or extinguished. You will take your place next to me until the end of the world."

Concerns of Elizabeth

The next day, I again felt this lack of a spiritual guide. Jesus spoke, "I leave you without a spiritual guide so your sufferings can merit many true spiritual guides for others. This, too, will be your missionary work."

On October 9, I asked that my children would always live in God's grace. Jesus responded, "When you are in heaven and see one of your children dying, you will go to their bed. Your drop of oil will fall and the Flame of Love will be lit. This will save their souls from damnation." Again, Satan attacked. "You are not bad. You are just terribly stubborn. Be convinced that you will never gain your goal. All will end in disgrace. Live a quiet, tranquil life. Why be a martyr? You will receive no reward."

The Communist Regime

Two days later, Jesus spoke about the consecrated religious who were scattered by the Communist regime. "Send this message to all who need to think about their vocation. Let them offer their sufferings to benefit souls. Those who cannot engage freely in apostolic activity should give themselves to a deep, spiritual life. This will produce abundant fruit. I count on their love."

In another message, he said, "To you who are lukewarm. How can I gain your attention? You no longer come to me in confidence. You are content with the passing things of earth, when I want you to come to me." After this, Jesus said to me, "Record my complaints. Perhaps, when they read it, their hard hearts will be inflamed. I wish I had to complain only about a few."

Completing the Task

On October 15, the Lord mentioned all of my difficulties, one by one and then said, "Do you want to abandon your difficulties? Let us suffer together. As yet, you have not completed any task." I could not record all he said. He speaks to me as we human beings speak with each other.

The Lord told me to meditate on "The Word became Flesh." I did this for months. What an indescribable miracle.

Three days later, Jesus warned me, "Satan and his forces want to destroy families. You are a mother and you know the many ways in which a family is torn apart. To save families, throw yourself into the furnace of suffering. How many sins come from destroyed families. Make reparation for these families."

While the Lord was speaking, I got out my little lunch. On Thursday and Friday, I fast on bread and water for the twelve priests. The Lord sat next to me (in a spiritual way). While we were eating, the Lord allowed me to feel his inner emotions, and said, "What would I not give to you? Just ask. I will compensate you for your poor lunch by my graces."

Pouring Out the Flame

On October 19th, Our Lady spoke, "My Flame of Love is burning. It is so great that I cannot keep it any longer within me. It leaps out to you with explosive power. When it pours out, my love will destroy the satanic hatred that contaminates the world. The greatest number of souls will be set free. Nothing like this has existed before. This is my greatest miracle that I will do for all. My words are crystal clear. Do not misinterpret them. Otherwise, you would be responsible. Act quickly, do not postpone my Cause for another day." Satan looked on with arms folded. He senses that the Flame of Love is already lit. This produced his terrible fury.

Describing the Flame

Our Lady continued, "Enter into battle. My Flame of Love will blind Satan to the degree that you spread it to the whole world. This Flame will work miracles in their hearts. They will communicate this miracle to others. No need for this miracle to be authenticated. I will authenticate the miracle in each soul. All will recognize the outpouring of the Flame of Love.

While saying this, Our Lady enlightened me about the mystery of the Word Became Flesh and spoke, "Always seek humility. Distance yourself from those who honor you." Then, the Lord spoke, "Have confidence. Always refer to the Flame of Love. The three divine persons are obligated to my Mother. All graces sought through her will be received. Her love warms the hearts of frozen souls."

The following week, Jesus spoke, "I am happy with this work. Do not be so ambitious. I am happy with little sacrifices. You think you will be a saint if you do great things. You are mistaken. Great things bring glory to you. We will gather small sacrifices."

The Important Petition

For a long time, I did not dare to record Our Lady's petition, "When you pray the Hail Mary, include the following petition, 'Spread the effect of grace of thy Flame of Love over all of humanity.'"

When the bishop asked why this should be done, Jesus explained, "Because of the Holy Virgin's efficacious pleas, the Most Blessed Trinity granted the outpouring of the Flame of Love. For her sake, you must place this prayer in the Hail Mary" (February 2, 1982).

Mary said, "I want to awaken humanity by this petition. This is not a new formula but a constant supplication." Then, Mary praised me, "I must praise you when I see you always busy with my Flame of Love. The Hungarian saints ask that my Flame of Love be lit as soon as possible in Hungary. The most powerful prayer is St. Emeric's intercession for youth." (Emeric was the son of St. Stephen, King of Hungary. He died as a youth in 1031.)

Our Lady's Promise

In November, when I asked for an outpouring of the Flame of Love for souls in purgatory, the Lord Jesus made me sense that a soul was freed. I felt indescribable relief and also the immeasurable happiness when the soul comes into God's presence. At the same time, my soul experienced the Lord's anguish.

Then, Our Lady spoke, "I grant your request. If at any moment, someone prays three Hail Mary's in my honor, while referring to the Flame of Love, they will free a soul from purgatory. During November, one Hail Mary will free ten souls. The souls in Purgatory should experience the effect of the Flame of Love."

Power Over Satan

On November 6 and 7, the devil tried to torture me, but he could not harm me. He was powerless and said, 'Now, it will be easy for you. You have slipped away from my claws." I did not understand how I could kneel for hours while the demon was so exasperated. Our Lady explained, "You have been filled with my Flame of Love. Through you, I will fill all souls. While someone is at adoration or visiting the Blessed Sacrament,

Satan loses his dominion. As a blind man, he ceases to rule over souls."

More Sacrifices

After this, the Blessed Virgin prepared me for more sufferings. However, this caused no fear. I possessed her Flame of Love. I was clothed with a great power that gave me almost superhuman strength.

On November 10, Jesus reminded me, "When you were working at the factory, you took a course on quality control and thought you would not pass the exam. You surprised yourself by becoming the top student. Even then, my hand was upon you.

"Later, you handled materials that hardened in the furnace. When some material was too hard, it needed to go back in and be melted again. I have melted you many times in the Flame of Love.

"You are my sunflower that produces oily seeds. The oil comes out only when the seeds are squeezed by sacrifices. This oil will fall on empty lamps and the Flame will be lit. It will even fall on souls that have no lamp (those without the light of true faith) and they will find the road to salvation."

Why Chosen

On November 19, Our Lady said, "I will tell you why I chose you as the first person entrusted with the Flame. Many souls are more worthy but the graces you received and the sufferings you have undertaken with such great fidelity have made you the chosen one.

"Your neighbors know and admire you. You have fought your battles before their eyes. I love to hear their good reports. I was attracted to you because you are not conceited.

"You are a mother of a large family and you know the pains and problems. You still experience many sorrows over your children. I have taken them all into consideration and shared with you the experiences of my Motherly heart.

"Many families in Hungary are like yours, very cold. I want to warm all families with my Flame of Love. I am the Sorrowful Mother and only a mother can share my sorrow. Be my eternal companion in lightening my sufferings."

Sent to A Priest

After entrusting the Flame to Father D., I thought I would find relief but the evil one humiliated me. So, on November 22, I went to Church at Mariaremete where I am quickly immersed in the Flame. Our Lady spoke, "We must seek lodging for My Flame of Love. Let's take action!" My heart shriveled up at the thought of these sufferings. She continued, "Right here in this church, you will spread the devotion." She directed me to a priest hearing confessions. I didn't even know him.

He asked why I was so restless and gave me five minutes to explain. I could not breathe rightly and had to speak slowly. I do not want to detail my torment. He told me I needed the cardinal virtue of prudence and agreed to receive the messages next Sunday. "You can bring them. I will read them but this does not mean that I am interested."

When I left the confessional, I thought about the cardinal virtues and said, "Jesus, I do not need the cardinal virtues to spread the Flame of Love. Otherwise, you would have told me."

Doubts About the Cause

The devil kept saying that I am deceiving myself and am filled with pride. I thought, "I should stop being involved in this Cause. I will admit my error to the priest and confess that all is a lie. I will recover my peace and be sincere."

At Communion time, I wondered if I should receive. "Jesus, I do not want to sin. How did I fall into this? Am I committing sin?" I remembered my childhood Catechism that to commit sin I had to knowingly and willingly offend God. I do not desire this sin, so I have not sinned.

At the Communion rail, the priest stopped in front of me. "Did he consider me unworthy?" He was just trying to separate two hosts. As he placed them on my tongue, they split apart, like two wings. I felt great relief, "O Lord, double your strength in me."

I knelt for a long time and it didn't seem like I was inventing the Flame of Love. "O Jesus, there is nothing in me that comes from me. Please accept me." He filled me with his presence and showed me the causes of these disturbances.

Another Promise

On another occasion, the Blessed Virgin promised, "If people assist at mass without any obligation and are in God's grace, I will pour out the Flame of Love and blind Satan during mass. When Satan is blinded, he can do nothing. Participating in mass helps the most in blinding Satan. He knows his downfall is near."

A Second Meeting

On November 29, I went to Father D, to whom I had given the messages a week ago. He had read only a few lines. "O Holy Virgin, what can I do? Nothing. This is not my fault." He talked about everything except the Flame of Love. I listened to his digressions and practiced control of my tongue. He admitted that what I said was true. His lack of confidence was painful. His skeptical words led me to say, "God sees my soul." The Blessed Virgin assured me that my sufferings promoted her Cause. The Lord said, "Do not be impatient with yourself. You must be detached from the priest's evaluation. I will compensate you with my graces."

Fridays

On Friday, I try to accept sacrifices generously. During the three hours of agony, I tried to dispose my soul for prayer. The Savior took compassion on me. "I was abandoned in towns and in cities. Now, failure fills my sublime being. Souls do not want to know me. They look at me for a moment and turn their head. Their compassion waits for another day. Oh, limitless indifference! My daughter, stay with me and relieve my sufferings by your presence. Do not leave me alone."

Going to the Bishop

On December 1, Our Lady spoke, "I will go with you. The priest to whom I send you will also suffer. He is tormented by doubts. You must pray and fast because I send you to those priests who have doubts. When they experience the Flame of Love, they will believe and trust in me." Our Lady asked, "Why are you afraid? (I was thinking about going to the bishop.) You have no reason to fear. We have prepared you. Fear just reflects your pride."

On December 12, the religious sister and I arrived in Szekesfelter at twilight. Snow covered the city. I thought of the Virgin's words, "We must find lodging for the Flame of Love." Then, she spoke, "Let us set out."

We went to the tomb of the saintly Jesuit priest, Stephen Kaszad, and then visited the tomb of the saintly bishop, Ottokar Prohaszka (1858-1927). While kneeling at his tomb, I was very touched. That night, I assisted at mass celebrated by the bishop.

The next morning, the bishop's secretary led us into the chapel, "O Jesus, we are finally here." Soon, the bishop came in and I knelt to make my confession. This lasted a long time. I admired his peace and self-control. He let me talk without any interruption. Then, he responded point by point, with extraordinary mental capacity. He calmed my soul and scattered my doubts. I kissed his hand and asked for his blessing. The Blessed Virgin spoke, "Rest now so that you have strength to continue the battle." For days, the bishop's blessing filled my heart with happiness.

Three days later, I awoke with my heart shaking from joy as I thought about the Flame of Love. Jesus spoke at mass. "Prepare for great sufferings. Now comes the persecution, just as Herod tried to kill me. Abandon yourself. I will give you the grace of full abandonment to me. This grace will totally control your being, and grace will go out to others. I had the bishop bless you as a reward for your sufferings, so he would know my divine will concerning you."

A Humiliation

On December 16, I returned to the priest and told him that I gave the messages to the bishop and told him the bishop's answers. "I would have said the same thing" he replied. By now, he had read the messages twice but did not understand them. I wanted to say some eloquent words, but I had no thoughts. He said that Friday and Saturday were already days of reparation, so this part was superfluous.

As I left the confessional, I was hurt. "Blessed Mother, the one you sent me to does not understand the Flame of Love." Terrible spiritual torments came over me. The Evil One raised new doubts. "This priest is very intelligent and he cannot understand your confused thoughts and tangled explanations. Only a disturbed person can believe this. Why do you keep trying?" My thoughts became confused. I thought I understood nothing. When I got home, I sang happy songs so my children would not see my depression.

The next day, Our Lady's words penetrated with deep kindness. "Why did you try so hard to say eloquent words? Remember, you are destined for suffering. Who understands my Flame of Love is not your concern. You cannot speak eloquent words. I am the one who confused you. Just enter into truth and be humble. Be careful in your temptations. The Evil One wants to shake your humility."

Back to the Priest

Since Father X was sick, I went back to Father D who said, "I was waiting for you." I said that I came because of sister's advice, not from my own will. When I spoke of the Cause, he had already forgotten much and admonished me, "God's Cause needs time to show its worth." He said he does not understand. I was not surprised. I told him that another priest had to read them twice and did not understand. However, I understand.

The priest said I should not force things. I told him the Cause does not depend on me. However, I have a strong inner drive to spread it. He said, "Be patient and God will clear the way." These efforts exhaust me. If it depended on me, I would not say one word. The voice that moves me belongs to the Blessed Virgin. She speaks without interruption and I cannot resist her urgency.

A major discussion began and I could not keep silent. What I said came from God. Finally, he said he would ask an opinion from another priest whose spiritual life was deeper.

Over the days, my torments grew less. As I was repairing the rug in the cold parish church, my hands were swollen from the cold and I thought of going home to get warm. Jesus said, "Why are you hurrying? Stay with me. No one comes to speak with me." After I finished the work, he spoke, "Your great and violent sufferings have exhausted you. Now I fill you with abundant grace. The rage of Satan is savage but he sees how great is the power of my grace in you."

After Father X had rejected me, the sister said, "Rejoice in this rejection." Jesus told me to esteem this grace of abandonment.

Chapter Three

1963

Early January at church, Jesus said, "Keep saying, 'My adorable Jesus.' This pleases me and gains graces for many souls." He stressed the word many.

During my evening meal I was restless, feeling that I had allowed myself too many comforts and yet, I cannot make more sacrifices. "Adorable Jesus, how silent you are in my soul."

Two days later, my daughter-in-law was weak, and I worked at her house before returning to my dwelling. Jesus spoke, "All morning you did not speak with me. I need to speak with you." Then, he complained bitterly, "In the whole parish, not one soul is adoring me now. So, I come to you and you will not reject me."

How Many Souls are Condemned

On January 8, while I was working, the Virgin spoke. "You are a mother. What if your six children were condemned to hell? What sorrow you would experience! Likewise, what torments I experience to see so many of my children fall into hell. Help me!" My heart cringed with sorrow.

Satan Attacks

The next day, Satan wanted me to abandon my new way of life. He used another strategy of smooth talk. "Give your message to everyone here. Do not keep it to yourself. Why do you not believe? You act like a coward. Announce this message everywhere."

The Lord said, "Pay no attention to his flatteries."

Later, Satan spoke of my failures, "You do not trust. Why do you go backwards? Give yourself to spreading the petition. You are a coward and worth nothing." I repelled his attacks by praying the Hail Mary.

A Letter to Sister

Because I could not get rid of these torments, I wrote a letter to the religious sister.

Dear Sister,

On Christmas night, I asked you if it was a sin to believe in the Cause. When you said, "No," I regained my peace. Later, new sufferings assaulted my soul. While my family slept in Christmas silence, I suffered with the Lord. A great insecurity came over me. This has constantly increased. I sob for hours. Some unknown power wants me to abandon my lies. I deceive others. The absolution I received from Father X is not valid because I have no desire to change. Without desire, absolution is worthless.

Whatever I told you before, do not believe. Everything is a lie. Darkness holds me captive and I cannot regain my peace until I withdraw all my lies. Yet, due to pride, I cannot do this. I am going to hell. There is no mercy for me. Please do not waste time on me. I might lose your friendship but I must make this retraction. Please free me from these inner torments. I feel I make sacrilegious Communions. I struggle in doubt.

Christ's voice in me is strong. "Do not look at me until you strip away your sins. I, too, abandon you. I do not need you. Depart from me. God has mercy only on the repentant sinner." I try in vain to bend my will. I find myself at the edge of condemnation.

For hours, I try to say the name of Jesus. I try pronouncing it letter by letter. A voice said, "Do not dare take this name on your lips."

Should I retract what I took to the bishop? Father D said my pride is wrapped in humility. He was right.

Sister, did a lie put these graces in my soul? How is this possible? How could I place myself so deeply in sin? When I go to Communion, I am a sacrilege.

Father X said, "Suffer gently" but my sins discourage me. My lie will not go away. I pray, "Heavenly Mother, help me to change. I am possessed by the devil and cannot renounce this lie." The inner voice accuses me, "You should have been interested in your own soul first." This is an infernal torment. Help me, Sister.

On January 14, the Lord spoke, "Make good use of this grace of abandonment. Satan wants to steal it from you. I permit these torments so he can see the power of abandonment." Satan tries to inject thoughts of pride. This is a terrible battle, giving me no peace. The Lord strengthened me with the penetrating look of his eyes. "Always look into my eyes. The look of my eyes will blind Satan."

Suffer Gently

I often remembered Father X's words, "Suffer gently." I receive new strength whenever I think of these words. Jesus said, "The words of Father X are also mine. Follow them in holy obedience." Sometimes, the torments are so great I can hardly think of the Flame of Love, as if Our Lady entrusted it to another. Possibly I am not fulfilling her petition. Did the Evil One take possession of me? Spiritual blindness keeps me in complete darkness.

Jesus spoke, "I will multiply and intensify your sufferings." I am so confused. I do not know what date it is. Satan tempted me with pride so Our Lady spoke, "You are the smallest one, the most ignorant with the least merits. But, through your humility, I want to send my messages." That I am the least is what I continually feel.

The Virgin spoke again, "People call me sorrowful mother, but I did not just suffer at the Cross. I am still suffering today."

The Lord's Glance

The next morning, I saw the Lord's penetrating glance. My bodily eyes cannot stand that glance. I shut my eyes tightly. His glance is like a flash of lightening which lights up everything. I saw all my sins. I cried for hours with greater sorrow than ever before. Jesus said, "Let our glances meld together so they form one glance." My sinful eyes will be one with his divine eyes. He wants this for everyone. He said, "Whoever walks with me will be joined with me in one glance."

At morning mass, this extraordinary gift left and Satan attacked. At the Consecration he was enraged, "Be a martyr. Sacrifice your life. Your Beloved sacrificed His. Throw your life away. End your atrocious torments. You must sacrifice your life sometime."

I called out, "Heavenly Father, you created me and determined the hour of my death. Free me from the Evil One. I am just a little spark who receives brilliance from your radiant glory. O Mary, blind Satan who wants to lead me into sin."

Satan had waged a foolish attack and did not know what to do. I always write "Satan" because he wants to conquer me and does not give this work to another.

Help From Father X

During these days, I went to confession to Father X. This always gains wonderful graces. Before confession, I was troubled by Satan. I said, "Father, I come here so you will help me to orient my spiritual state." He said he would clarify God's will for me. I calmed down and experienced a day of joy.

For some months now, Jesus keeps saying, "Never leave me alone without your sufferings." Then, he said, "Your sufferings will go beyond all that you have suffered until now." Happiness filled my soul. He had wanted to place my soul in a furnace of sufferings. Now, he has arranged this.

I am continually fighting. Part of me wants to spread the messages and another voice says, "Burn them. Throw them into the fire." I thought of Father X, "Do not allow these disturbing thoughts to come close to you."

The next day, Jesus said, "Do not set aside my request." Then, Our Lady spoke, "To resist my words comes from human doubts. Put them away. They will destroy your abandonment."

Spreading the Flame

The Flame of Love fills my whole being and my soul is filled with a marvelous perception. We have no reason to worry. We are small instruments.

On February 1, Jesus said, "Stay next to me and suffer with me." A spiritual power filled my soul with a burning desire from the Flame of Love. I thought, "What if the Virgin's Flame of Love ceased to flood me with its grace?" I realized how deprived are people who do not have this outpouring. An unimaginable force increased my desire to spread the Flame.

Rejected By Others

On February 4, Jesus said, "Many whom I love will treat you with suspicion and will set you aside. Come with me to Calvary. Our Mother comes with us. You are her chosen Carmelite and I can refuse her nothing because she speaks of her Flame of Love. I asked my disciples to pray with me in the Garden. They did not, so the Father sent an angel.

"Do not withdraw, even if Satan's torments increase. His power extends only as far as I permit."

At mass, Satan again tortured me claiming that he had power over me and could possess me. Instead, he prefers to continually torment me. These sufferings exhaust my whole being.

In the afternoon of February 7, the Blessed Virgin urged me again to spread her Flame of Love. Every humiliation will help the Cause.

Because I relaxed after Satan's trials, Jesus said, "You are too immersed in earthly things. In your battles, do not seek relief by looking to earth. Come closer to me. Always look up. I and my Mother await you in heaven."

The Lord's Comforts

I write this to show how the Lord's goodness comforts me in difficult hours.

On February 9, Jesus said, "I will increase your sufferings until martyrdom." As I reflected on these words, he said this three more times. I prayed, "O my Mother, thank you for these sufferings by which I can advance your holy Cause."

The next day, the church was cold and I wanted to finish my prayers before it got dark. Jesus begged me to stay. "Do not leave me here. I am alone and without consolation. How often I am alone. I share this Church with you. You enter whenever you wish. Did you see anyone else?" "No one, Lord. During this time, I saw no one."

Jesus responded, "You see why I say, 'Do not leave me alone.' I will accompany you with the penetrating glance of my eyes." Because of his love, the cold and the tiredness ceased.

Family Blessings

Our Lady said that the Flame of Love protected my family. The Evil One could not lead them into sin. Jesus said, "Because of my Mother's prayer, I was here all night blessing your family. How much we love you."

My daughter was sick and I thought of going to the doctor. The Lord said, "Do not go anywhere. It will be better if your daughter is not cured." I grew depressed because she has a husband and a child. Jesus told me why, "Your daughter always has temptations. By a long sickness, I will fill her with abundant graces and her soul will be purified."

A Mystical Grace – Flight of the Spirit

In mid-February, the Lord filled me with such peace, I could not speak. I have no name for this marvelous grace which kept increasing and lifted me up from the earth. When I could finally speak, I said, "Lord Jesus, what are you doing with such an unworthy person?" With one breath, he had lifted my soul by a direct flight to the infinite love of his Divine Being. The Lord spoke, "I do this because I love you very much."

My soul was so united to him. It was as if I left my earthly existence. Although I had to care for my sick daughter, nothing disturbed my union with God. It was like floating in some high place and looking down on my body's activity. This grace kept increasing like waves upon my soul, which was flying high in its nearness to God.

These graces totally saturate my soul. Even while I do my chores. The Lord spoke, "Yesterday, you were allowed into the nearness of God as if you had taken flight from the earth. This is a reward. By perseverance, you will always arrive at a higher level of grace. Live a holier life and I will intensify the graces."

Returning to Father X

On March 11, Our Lady spoke, "In spite of everything, my Flame will be enkindled. We will permit Satan to use all kinds of temptations against those who want to put into practice my Flame of Love. We have no time to lose. A definite time has been determined for the Flame to be lit. Satan needs to test the twelve priestly souls. I will help them gain victory." Many times, the Blessed Virgin told me to go to Father X. The religious sister told me to obey. Nothing can hold me back.

On March 23, I went to Father X and gave him the message but he still does not want to be my director. He feels he lacks strength due to his latest illness. Also, he has doubts about the Cause. He said I am stubborn, inflexible and attached to my own will. I told him I have no strength and that I came to him only by heaven's invitation. My impatience does not come from my will. I have no personal interest in all of this. He just said, "Fine."

If he did not want to be my director, he should send me to another. He just said, "Somehow it will happen." At the end, he said "I bless you very much." I left in peace.

However, since this priest did not believe, new doubts arose. His rejection was humiliating. So, I complained to the Lord.

Effects of the Rejection

The next day, my soul was shaken by this rejection. Then, the Lord spoke, "Do you believe in this Cause? Tell me." "Lord, you know my faith better than I do." He responded, "You are an instrument in our hands. Your place is next to the Mother of Sorrows. Do you want to continue to be our instrument?

"The priest shook you by not believing your sincere words. This suffering is just a rehearsal for the future. This time of grace for the whole world is a holy Cause, but you cannot have feet of clay. To put this into action, your soul must be strong like steel." The Lord's words gave me faith and confidence. Without these two, no virtue can take root.

The Lord's Teachings

On March 27, the Lord said that the Spirit of Pentecost will flood the earth with his power and a great miracle will gain the attention of all humanity. This will be the effect of grace of the Flame of Love.

Due to lack of faith, earth is entering into darkness, but earth will experience a great jolt of faith. People will believe and will create a new world. By the Flame of Love, confidence and faith will take root. The face of the earth will be renewed because "something like this has not happened since the Word became Flesh." Earth, although flooded with sufferings, will be renewed by Our Lady's intercession.

The Lord asked me to take the messages to the bishop. Since the bishop was confirming nearby, I went to ask for an appointment. He told me to come to his home. I spoke with him for an hour and gave him the messages.

A Teaching

In May, Jesus said, "You are my little drop of water. Immerse yourself in the intoxicating wine of my divinity. Have just one thought: the salvation of souls. I only want flowers that are cut. Those followers which are still in a pot represent a soul which still draws its strength from earth."

Communicating An Experience of God's Fire

The Lord asked me to record the following experience. While praying before the altar, I was taken up in the fire of God's love. When a religious sister came near me, she was wrapped in the same fire. God's presence filled her for weeks.

On another occasion, when I met a priest in the street, the Divine Presence flowed out and filled him. To another priest, this happened on numerous occasions. When these outpourings happen, I am overwhelmed. Jesus said, "Through you, I give these same graces. The Flame of Love forces me to do so."

The Earth's Terrible Situation

On May 19, Jesus said, "When you were born, I wrote 'suffering' on your life's story. I will continue to write this word until the day you die. In heaven, I will reveal your life like a movie. Through the Spirit's illumination, your soul will be plunged into a beautiful ecstasy."

Our Lady continued the teaching. "Earth is experiencing the calm before the storm, like a volcano about to explode. Earth is now in this terrible situation. The crater of hatred is boiling. I, the beautiful Ray of Dawn, will blind Satan. No dying soul should be condemned. My Flame of Love will now be lit. It will be a terrible storm, a hurricane that will want to destroy faith. In that dark night, heaven and earth will be illuminated by the Flame of Love that I offer to souls.

"Just as Herod persecuted my Son, so the cowards, the cautious and the lazy extinguish my Flame of Love. The heavenly Father protected the child Jesus and he will defend my Flame of Love. I lead to heaven those whom my Son gained by his immense sorrow."

The Blessed Virgin is the most powerful Sovereign in the whole world. She is the Queen, filled with the majesty of someone who is totally determined. Suddenly, she spoke in a motherly voice, "You must put this into practice. Do not fear, my little instrument."

Answered Prayers

On May 24, I prayed for a soul that was gravely ill and had not been to confession in ten years. Then I heard that she had received the sacraments. The Lord spoke, "Have you ever asked for souls and I did not grant it? Never grow tired of asking for souls. If many asked, many would be converted. Especially the sick must ask. Their one petition can bring about massive conversions."

A month later, I went to a neurologist. I could tell that he was a very spiritual man, so I revealed my spiritual life. I spoke about another doctor who had lived years without the Sacrament of Matrimony and how the Lord Jesus promised me that he would not be condemned. We spoke for two hours. He will send a report.

Consolation In Sufferings

On July 24, I was thinking about the many sufferings that fill my body and soul. The Virgin spoke, "Suffer with perseverance and devotion. Time is short and never returns. What you do not accept at a given moment, never returns. Every small drop of sacrifice accepted with love delights the Holy Trinity."

Two days later, the Lord spoke, "I must complain again. Souls created in my Father's image and likeness fall into Satan's hands and he drags them to hell. The Flame of Love calms my sorrow. Accept all the sufferings that I send to you."

Our Lady spoke, "Do not abandon the battle. By my Flame of Love, a new era of grace, never before known on the earth, will begin."

On August 1, while working in the kitchen, the Lord spoke. However, when family members came in, he kept silent. He is infinite kindness. At 2:40 I looked at my watch. Once, the Lord had said that the final twenty minutes on the cross were his worst agony.

Three days later he said, "When the effect of grace of my Mother's Flame of Love pours out into all hearts, she will be venerated as never before. All will join in one gigantic prayer of petition. Give my messages to those in authority and tell them not to impede My Mother who wants to pour out the Flame of Love."

On August 7, the Lord said, "I am continually at your disposal. You do not need to stand in line or to have an appointment. I am present everywhere. Repentance is the only step that comes near to me. Do not wander. Stay at my side so I can quickly lift you up from any fall."

Instructions for Elizabeth

Toward the end of August, I asked the Lord if He had truly sent me to Father X to be my director because Father X had often rejected this role. Jesus spoke, "The priest to whom I sent you has a free will. He has doubts and does not see the matter clearly. As yet, he has made no firm decision, but he will see that all is authentic. He, too, will suffer. That is the only way to be worthy to serve our Cause."

Our Lady said, "In September, you must begin to spread the Flame of Love even more. Give my message to the bishop. Respond to any question and be humble." (My confessor did not let me go to the bishop.)

Later, the Lord said, "Record my words the best you can. No need for neatness and spelling. Do nothing that would make you look intelligent. Through your humility, we want to put Our Cause into action."

On August 31, I stayed after the evening mass and the sister sacristan locked the Church, not knowing I was still inside. As I interceded for the souls in purgatory, Our Lady spoke, "I value your longing for the souls in purgatory. Until now, you had to say three Hail Marys to free one soul. In the future, three Hail Marys will free ten souls from that place of suffering."

Sacrifices

On September 10, the Savior asked me to fast on bread and water each Monday to free a priest soul from purgatory. The fast weakens me but I can still do my housework. At night, I was very emotional and ate my little dinner of bread in his presence. He said, "I will stay with you a few more minutes. Feel my blessed Presence." Then, he said, "Rest in peace. I am going to look for hearts." I asked, "Where are you going?" "To visit my consecrated souls and offer my graces, again."

At lunch, I began to read a magazine article. The Lord spoke, "I wanted you to renounce all distracting literature. Your life is prayer and sacrifice. Do not fear. I will repay you."

Help For the Dying

In September, the Blessed Virgin asked me to suffer the agony of the dying. She said, "If my Flame of Love is lit upon the earth, grace will be poured out upon the dying. Satan will be blinded and through your nightly vigil, the agony of the dying will end. Even the hardened sinner will have a conversion." As she spoke, my own sufferings increased and I almost died from the pain.

Going to the Bishop

Two days ago, when I gave Our Lady's request to my director, he told me not to go to the bishop and he would take responsibility. I told him that I will obey him but the Blessed Virgin will keep urging me. Today I heard her say, "Go, quickly." "Mother, in what direction do I go and to whom?" She clearly responded, "Go to Father E and ask him when the bishop will come."

I foresaw great difficulties. What would Father E say? But I could not resist, so I went to him. He said, "The bishop will come here on Monday. I asked the exact time so I could see him. Even though the inspiration was true, the anguish of doubts still continued.

Our Lady spoke again, "I extend the Flame of Love over all towns, not just those that live in Holy Mother the Church, also on all souls that have been baptized. (The diary notes that this was further extended by Our Lady to the non-baptized. September 19 and 22, 1963)

Family Holy Hour

On September 24, Our Lady spoke, "My Flame of Love extends to the souls in purgatory. Write down my words and give them to those in authority. "If a family keeps a holy hour on Thursday or Friday, if someone in that family dies, the person will be freed from Purgatory after one day of the fast kept by a family member."

The Lord spoke, "You still have your intense personality. If you surrender this, I will make of you a work of art. Be like grapes transformed into wine from which comes the Precious Blood. Whomever God resides in will be divinized."

On October 2, the Lord said, "Do not let the world attract you. You have become an arrow that flies straight to me. I can hardly wait for you to come to heaven."

Our Lady's Pleas

On October 18, Our Lady said, "Only a mother can understand my anguish. How many of my children will be condemned? I collapse beneath the weight of this sorrow." She again asked me to make every effort. I must take up her Cause. She added, "Hurry. Each minute means the loss of souls. Do not be trapped by feelings of doubt. I will take the Cause to those who can advance it quickly."

Yet, I doubted. "Mother, I have taken so many initiatives, yet everything remains the same. Please take everything from me because I am the victim of my own imaginings." She answered, "Believe in my power." Her request echoes in my soul and I know I must begin.

Mystical Experiences

In late October, my guardian angel told me to adore the Holy Trinity. So, I put my housework aside and went to my little dwelling. All human words completely fail to describe my experiences. All my past experiences seemed dull and dark compared to the Trinity. I spent two days immersed in the Trinity. Yet I could not free myself from doubts that I am the foolish victim of my imagination. My spiritual director would explain these doubts but, right now, I cannot go to him. It was like climbing a pole. I would either get to the top or fall off. Only the experiences of the Blessed Trinity kept me from abandoning the battle.

Ecstasy

That night the Spirit of Love filled me (and I must write this clearly). All feeling of time and space ceased. In ecstasy, the Lord's voice gave me extraordinary strength, "After each great battle, the Holy Trinity took greater possession of your soul and I have brought this to the highest possible level. You will now be frequently lifted up to the Father. I will speak less often because your frequent immersion in the Trinity will lift you closer to God and you will remain in the heavenly Father's company.

"This is the reward of your sufferings. Now, you will fight an uninterrupted battle with your body. You must fight these earthly attractions to keep possession of the Spirit of Love. I will apply your merits to the twelve priests who will put the Flame of Love into action."

In Church, I asked, "Lord, are there any words that come from my imagination? This doubt causes me unrest." Jesus said, "You have no reason to think that."

Need for Urgency

In November, the Blessed Virgin continually urged new initiatives. "I can no longer contain the Flame of Love in my heart. Let it leap out to everyone. Prepare to set out. Only the first step is difficult. After that, My Flame of Love will encounter no resistance and will illuminate souls with a gentle light. They will be intoxicated with abundant graces and announce the Flame to everyone. A torrent of graces which have not been given since the Word became Flesh will pour out."

The Virgin kept insisting, "Take up my Cause. You cannot rest. Do not be tired. Do not give up. All interested in my Cause must come together." She kept insisting, "Do this. I am the one who urges you."

Total Dedication

On November 27, she complained, "Many will come and do nothing. I will demand an accounting from whomever places obstacles. Defend my Cause from all obstacles. Dedicate yourselves to blind Satan. We need all the forces in the world to do this. Do not delay. You have responsibility for many souls. I do not want even one soul to be condemned. This responsibility does not just fall upon priests. The responsibility is great but the work will not be in vain. Satan will be humiliated and unable to exercise his power. Do not prolong this beginning period." Again, she asked me to take the messages to the bishop.

A Letter to Father X

The next day, the Blessed Virgin insisted that I take this letter to Father X.

Dear Father,

Do not be upset by this letter. I am just a small instrument. I do whatever Our Lady tells me. I will also obey you and do all that you tell me. I am exhausted. The Virgin's urgings never cease. She asks that the petition be sent to the bishop. He welcomed her Flame of Love. I can only write the words she dictated.

When I spoke with the bishop, he said, "Get a regular spiritual director. He will know what to do. If he comes to me, I will talk with him." Father, you must speak with the bishop. The Blessed Virgin asks that you meet as soon as possible. These are her constant pleas.

Do Not Be Passive

On December 2, Our Lady was very clear, "Do not be passive about my sacred Cause. Through a few people, a great outpouring of graces will change the world. No one must excuse themselves or refuse my invitation. All are my instruments. (I wrote this to Father X, also.)

A week later, Our Lady sent me to Father E so he would go to Father X. I cannot write what the Blessed Virgin said during the ecstasy. She fills me with a special love.

Cleaning Behind the Altar

On December 15, the Lord Jesus instructed me, "I want followers who will imitate my sacrifices. As a man, I experienced every type of suffering. Your own loving commitment still touches me. When I encounter one holy person, I pardon many. Do penance, so my hope in you produces salvation. What will I not grant to you? Your sufferings have widened your soul and all my gifts now fit. You will bring to heaven a multitude of souls."

Afterward, I began to clean behind the altar where there was a thick layer of dust. The Lord spoke, "Many souls are like this altar, allowing dust to gather for years. These souls are gray and dusty. By their bad example, many, many souls are soiled. They do not realize this and they avoid what is difficult.

"These souls know much but they do not experience me. They give me only the crumbs, what they do not need. Yet, they think they deserve a reward. These souls enjoy my kindness but never think of what they should do in return. This is the pain in my soul.

"I complain to you because a shared sorrow is half a sorrow. Whoever is covered with dust does not have the light. Let us pray for these dusty souls." The Lord revealed a priestly soul for whom I must sacrifice. He is avoiding his chosen task. I was shocked by this revelation.

Chapter Four

1964

Lukewarmness

On the first Sunday, I went to the hospital to visit my child. Later, it was cold and I could hardly walk. However, I wanted to be present for the 5:00 PM community adoration. Overcoming the numbness in my feet, I hurried to church. Jesus spoke, "You try so hard to please me. This will gain a torrent of graces."

During adoration, he asked me to pray for those who have not repented of their sins. Thinking of my own sins, I began to cry. The Lord spoke, "The world is in darkness because consecrated souls are lukewarm. They do not understand how dangerous lukewarmness is. Tell Father X that he and all spiritual guides must see the importance of inspirations. Without these, no one can lead a spiritual life. The souls they guide will wither."

The Lord Forewarns

On January 13, the Lord warned me, "Be careful, Elizabeth. Your soul will be a battleground. Satan will attack your humility. He will make you unsure. He wants to deceive you so you abandon your humble task." A few hours later, the troubles began. I could not expel these revolting thoughts. I would not have remained stable except that the Lord forewarned me.

On January 15, the Lord said, "Anyone can read my words but only those who come to me can understand my longing to save souls. Give yourself to this goal. Believe the words, 'If each Christian saved just one soul, no one would be lost.'" Then Our Lady spoke, "I do not want one soul condemned. All must desire the same thing. That is why I place this beam of light, the Flame of Love, in your hands."

The next day, the Lord said, "I am the blood donor to the world. My Precious Blood is warm and gives movement to frozen, paralyzed souls. By my Divine Blood, all can become divine. Why would souls want to be ordinary? My table is always set. I, the host, have sacrificed everything. Let sacrificial charity lead all to my table. When will they finally come to me?" These mystical experiences keep my soul in a great spiritual state and the Evil One can do nothing.

Some Words for Mothers

The next day, the Lord spoke about his home in Nazareth. "In this home, I prepared for sacrifices. You were an orphan. So, it was your marriage home that prepared you. You needed this family setting to mature. In misfortunes, people return home to be comforted.

"You, mothers, must extend the warmth of your homes even to those children who are now grown. You must imitate my Mother who always provided me with her love. Her powerful intercession gained this great grace for all of you. She does not want to perform a public miracle. (This happens at her great shrines.) Rather, she wants every family to be a sanctuary where she works miracles in the hearts. She places in your hands the Flame of Love which will blind Satan who wants to rule over families."

Then the Virgin spoke. "My anguish comes from the danger that threatens the whole world because families are no longer places of prayer. I want to save the world and I want you to be the first to experience this immense power to blind Satan. You will receive the great grace by which we will save souls from eternal condemnation."

Passing Diversions

The religious sister was listening to a beautiful concert. Then, she gave me the hearing device. I immediately became absorbed in the music. The Lord spoke in soft words, "Am I not jealous of you during these few minutes?" His words drowned out the beauty of the music, "Renounce your own entertainment. Do not allow any passing diversion. For you, only one thing is necessary—to share in my saving work. Do not say that I am very strict. You must renounce yourself moment by moment. You cannot stop even for a short time. All passes away. Only your work for souls remains."

Experiences in the Snow

The chilblains in my feet began to bother me again. So I spent the afternoon inside, until I heard some footsteps in the snow. I went out to see and had walked just a few steps when the Lord allowed me to experience his presence at my side. My whole body shook. My strength abandoned me. This grace went beyond all others. I do not know how I experienced the touch of his garments. As I returned inside, I realized how long I had been gone. The Lord spoke, "Since you could not come to Church, I came to you. Oh, the lowliness and the coldness that always surrounds me. That is why I stay close to you. I will stay for a long time. What else will I do with myself? No one else comes to adore me. I gave you the sacred trembling as your reward."

The next day, Jesus promised, "anyone who reads about what I gave you yesterday will share, without any exceptions, in the outpouring of my graces. By this, I pay you in advance for all your sufferings."

Explaining the Ecstasies

A few days later, Jesus explained this experience, "Do not try to understand what has happened. You have traveled this road in a short time. Even the saints are in admiration. With my love, I have lifted you up and you fly like an arrow to me.

"If I lift you to myself, do not even reflect on it. Don't try to understand. Your intellect cannot understand my lifting you from this earth in these ecstasies. I did not give you a spiritual director at first because I wanted to train you for your destiny. Accept the guidance of your director. All he says comes from my inspiration."

First Friday (February)

The flu still tortures me with pain in my eyes and face. The fever consumes me. In the morning, the Lord said, "Welcome, my daughter." He allowed me to hear the beating of his heart, which I know well. He said, "This first Thursday and Friday will be good days. People will make reparation and graces will fall upon dry and confused souls. Ask me for these souls. Results do not matter. The continual desire to do my will is what makes a saint. Loving me again and again is important. This effort dispels my pain. What you give me each day is not important. It is only important that you never stop giving."

The Blank Check

"Let my Precious Blood fall upon you. My drops of Blood are a bank check. The check is valid until the end of the world. The soul in God's grace can cash it at any time before their death. Each soul must use this check as frequently as possible. It is the ransom paid by my Precious Blood. If put off until the end, the time will be short to gain its full value. Take advantage while you still have your full vigor."

On February 8, the Lord showed me a rotating picture. On every side were innumerable souls. They were suffering in soul and in body. The Lord spoke, "This shows you how great is the harvest and how scarce are the workers. Keep working for souls. Put all your efforts into this work."

Writing Everything

A few days later, I resolved to write down everything that happened this year. Before, I thought that some experiences were just for me but the Lord insisted that I write everything. He gives graces through me and even with the personal stories I help others. Because of lack of schooling, it is not easy for me to write or to spell. So, I keep much stored in memory. But now, I will try to write everything.

Iron In The Fire

Last Thursday, my fast day, I had pain in my ear and throat. Seeing my painful efforts to fast, the Lord said, "Since the two of us are so exhausted, let us eat something hot." After having hot soup, I felt better. The Lord said, "We have both gained strength. What would you do if I left you alone? I will never do that."

The next day, the Lord said, "By the Flame of divine Love I will expand your soul to receive more abundant graces. Heat expands iron and allows it to be formed. So, as you draw near to the burning fire of my humanity, I will form your soul according to my plan."

The next morning, as I came home from mass, Jesus continued, "I pour over you the burning fire of my love and you must suffer all the way to martyrdom. Accept my words as a definitive proof of my divine love."

On February 17, the Lord said, "You are really very weak. The world must see that the divine will is manifested through the weak. Experiencing your weakness is no obstacle. The Cause only needs your humility to succeed."

A Special Priest

What I write is special. The Blessed Virgin led me to give the Flame of Love to a priest whom I did not know. In the sacristy, I learned his name and address, but I felt restless, as if this information was not correct. Our Lady said, "Go and learn immediately the priest's correct name and address." I returned to the confessional lines but the priest was not there. Surprisingly, he returned and I knew our Lady had inspired me.

I entered his confessional and told him that I had written down these extraordinary happenings for him to read. He remembered, "It treats about blinding Satan." He said he would pray for the Cause. What surprised me was that this priest understood the central message, "to blind Satan," the only purpose of the Flame of Love. When the priest told me his name and address, I knew Our Lady had inspired me because it was different from the one given in the sacristy.

An Echo of Praise

On February 25, at the nighttime adoration, I said, "Jesus, I live and I die for you." The Lord said the same thing. He returned all my prayers like an echo. I prayed, "I adore you. I bless you. I exalt you." The Lord said, "For this great praise, I bless you." Possibly I misunderstood and was about to erase these words. The Lord said, "Do not do that. I give everything to a soul that returns my love. I allow my heart to be driven by madness."

On February 29, I prayed, "Adorable Jesus, accept me as I am." He said, "You must also accept me with my beaten body and pierced hands, feet and heart. I sacrificed Myself. You can never do too much for me."

On May 24, 1963 I had transcribed Jesus' teaching that all can share in this redeeming work, even the sick. Today he said, "Because that teaching is very important, I will repeat it. I speak to all mothers. Your work is very important. You are called to populate my Kingdom and to fill the places of the fallen angels. All progress in my Church begins in your wombs. You have the greatest work that requires the greatest responsibility."

Various Petitions

I was praying, "Blessed be Jesus Christ, true God and true man." The Lord interrupted me. "I am both true God and true man. As God, I penetrate your heart. As man, I speak to you. Our hearts beat as one and you share in my divinity. All who are one with me receive this sharing, which is an eternal circular movement between heaven and earth. Your sacrifices rise to me and my blessings pour out upon you."

A few days later, I prayed for my family. The Lord said, "Elizabeth, can you imagine me not granting you something for the good of souls? I would be opposing my saving work. Just make sacrifices for those whom you want to lead along my road."

Later, the Lord said, "Concentrate on priestly vocations, those who have not yet accepted their call and those who are already priests."

Laziness

At night, the Lord said, "The great storm is coming and it will carry away indifferent souls who are consumed by laziness. The great danger will erupt when I take away my hand of protection. Warn everyone, especially the priests, so they are shaken out of their indifference."

The Lord taught me about desires. "To desire requires sacrifices. A child perseveres in his studies to be an excellent pupil. The athlete who wants to win accepts every sacrifice. The father makes many sacrifices to have his family. Desires and sacrifices are inseparable."

Stripping Satan of His Powers

On March 17, I was enjoying the solitude of my dwelling, when the door opened and I sensed the Evil One's presence. "I have come to see how you are doing." He could speak little because he was stripped of his powers and blinded. He was forced to remain close to me. I said, "You have no power to harm me." He replied, "What will you do in this hour of quiet?" "I will adore God for all those whom you have turned aside." He was pained but forced to listen to me. "God pardons every repentant sinner. If you would rid yourself of your pride and repent, God would pardon you. But you hold on to your pride and you must suffer. Soon, you will be blind and stripped of all power. This pains you but it is true." He had no answer. His powers were gone. Satan disappeared without a trace.

Some Words of the Lord

The next day, the Lord said, "Those who truly love need only a few words. Place your head on my heart to gain strength for future battles. I await sacrifices from many but only a few respond."

After some days of fasting, I ate, but only for nourishment. The Lord said, "Taking your food without any taste is a sacrifice which is tasty for me. We harvest together."

I asked the Lord if I could publish these messages during my lifetime. He gently answered, "Why even ask? It is like asking if you can share in my redeeming work during your lifetime. What am I constantly urging you to do? I lifted you up like an arrow so you can spread my messages as soon as possible. My pleas stress the urgent importance of the Cause." Three times, the Lord asked me to send the messages to my spiritual director.

Holy Thursday

I wanted to spend the night in Church but this was impossible. The Lord said, "I will await you when you arrive home." When I entered my dwelling, He made his presence felt. Then, he filled me with anguish and sorrow. I had to hold on so I would not collapse. The Lord spoke, "I lived in fear of this night in Gethsemane. It is an honor to share in my sorrow. This is a sign that you share in my work."

When midnight came, I had to gather my strength because I had had no rest. I only persevered fifteen minutes in my kneeling position. The suffering totally weakened me. I went to bed but could not sleep. On Friday, Our Lord said, "Do not withdraw. Suffer with me all day."

Easter Monday Homily

Today, Father E preached the best sermon I have ever heard. The Lord said, "I flooded the priest with abundant graces. Tears flowed and hearts were moved. You see the fruits of your work. You have been my parish representative. These are the results."

Father E spoke about hope and told the story of a young soldier who was wounded and had no hope to live. After his confession, he asked the priest to sing a hymn to the Blessed Sacrament with him. The soldier said, "How happy I am to come to know the Lord." As Father told the story, God's grace poured out and tears flowed from everyone's eyes.

Early April

The Lord said, "Patience, perseverance and fidelity keep you close to me. You and the others will see what no human eye has seen and no ear has heard. In heaven, we will see and hear as one."

A few days later, he said, "Elizabeth, you are a broom in my hands by which I sweep everywhere. By accepting sacrifices, you become worthy of being taken up by my hand. When it comes to serving me, no one can do too much."

A Special Promise

On April 14, when I arrived home from church, the Lord was waiting, "At your request, I am blessing your family and the whole neighborhood. Your children's salvation is assured. I will stay in your dwelling because I enjoy the silence of your little room. I find it difficult to be without you. You feel the same. We await the moment when nothing will separate us. In heaven, we will be totally one."

The next day, the Blessed Virgin awoke me at midnight in a special way. I wasn't tired, even though I had only one hour of sleep. I was still overwhelmed by the Lord's promise that from now on he would always wait for me in my room.

"Adorable Jesus, since words never come to my lips, I constantly shed tears of thanksgiving. Tears are the music of my heart and my only gift. I want to place my sorrow in each grain of dust so the wind can take them to you. This is my hymn, my poem and my music." The Lord said, "Your profound sorrow will lead many to repent and to come to me."

Delivering the Messages

On April 18, the Lord said, "Tell your confessor to send the material, so the messages about the Cause reach the Holy Father by Pentecost, 1965. My Mother's messages are urgent. Do not set them aside." His powerful words caused me to tremble. I must deliver God's words quickly. Can anyone accept this task without trembling? I have no doubts. The Lord took them all away.

Our Lady said, "Use your sacrifices to stir up the Flame of Love. Do not allow the flame to flicker. Use well the time given to you.

Agony and Ecstasy

I am happy to keep the strict fast on Monday because it frees one priestly soul from purgatory. The Lord said, "Because of your firm determination to keep the fast, I will free one priestly soul every hour beginning at midnight." When I heard this, I began to experience the suffering that these souls endure before coming into God's presence. It lasted just a few minutes. After Communion, I experienced the joy of that priest entering heaven. I trembled from this ecstasy of grace and felt free from the earth's gravitational pull.

Experiencing The Trinity

On May 28, before going to bed, I prostrated before the image of his Sacred Face. I felt an extraordinary outpouring of God's Majesty. During that instant, earth ceased to exist for me. I was entirely in the presence of God. The next day, the Lord explained that I had experienced the Holy Trinity. The Lord said, "This was only for an instant because you could not withstand this experience while still on earth."

Spreading the Cause

On June 15, the Lord commanded, "The spreading of the Flame of Love must be the main purpose of your life. Let it flow smoothly like a stream of water, which nothing can stop. This purifying grace saves and gives life. Tell this to your spiritual Father. I want him to put it into action."

Two days later, after a great interior battle, I went to my director. Again, he will take no steps until he experiences something in his soul. His words caused new sufferings. Two weeks later, the Lord said, "It is urgent for you to go to your director. I am prompting him to speak with Father E." Our Lady added, "You must go. Your humiliation actually moves the Cause ahead."

In the morning of June 29, before the tabernacle I heard the Lord speak, "My Elizabeth, how I have waited for you. I knew you would be the first to come. I delight to be with the children of men. Unfortunately, I am welcomed by few. I want to give an increased measure of love, unknown until now. Accepting this grace demands great sacrifice. What value would this Cause have if there were no battle? Always try to go higher. Do not look to the right or the left. Look only into my eyes."

Reprimand and Promise

I was in a drugstore waiting for some medicines, when I started to read a few lines in the paper. The Lord made his request. "Realize that this short time is useful. Put aside the newspaper and help suffering souls to come to heaven. Write this down. All can help in my eternal plans."

On July 27, the Lord said, "Your little room is my tabernacle and I enjoy being with you. I gave you a place in my church. So, you provide me with a home. Let me explain your great capacity. You inebriate the all-powerful God. All can make God happy by repentance for their sins."

On August 3 the Lord said, "Just as a magnet attracts and never lets go, so I never let go of anyone. Let us pray for God's mercy for those who tear themselves away from this divine attraction."

Going to the Confessor

After a long time, I finally got to confession and told my spiritual Father that my soul was tormented because I was proud, untruthful, and deceiving him. I have had no peace.

He calmed me down and said that these accusations came from the devil and are not true. I need only be obedient and sincere, revealing to him all my future difficulties.

Two days later, Jesus promised, "I will give light to your confessor and, in the future, he will see that the Cause is authentic. After a

short rest, I will intensify your sufferings. Will you accept this?"
"O Lord Jesus, you seek my total surrender. I live only for you.
I want to love you as no repentant sinner has ever loved you."

The Lord said, "Elizabeth, repeat those words. They delight
me. How I suffer from those who reject me. Tell me, is it
difficult to love me?" When I responded by my sorrow for sin,
the Lord said, "Your sorrow is like a bee that gathers honey.
You pray for souls and they repent of their sins. The bee must
work. Otherwise, the bee and the flower are useless. Nothing
happens. Just as the collected pollen becomes honey, so your
tears become honey in souls."

On August 18, the Lord said, "You constantly adore me. How
I wish there were many of you. I thirst for your words because
they quench my yearning for souls. On the cross, I exclaimed,
'I thirst.' I say the same to consecrated souls."

On August 22, he said, "Elizabeth, I love you and I make this
confession. I seriously want you to return my love. Love, filled
with repentance, intoxicates me. Let everyone's repentant love
intoxicate me."

Why Elizabeth Was Chosen

On August 27, Our Lady explained, "I chose a Mother to
transmit my messages because only a mother can experience
my feelings. Without maternal experiences, you could not
make great sacrifices. Motherhood is a vocation saturated with
sufferings. As a Mother, I guarantee your heavenly reward."

Three days later, a newspaper fell into my hands. After I read a
few words, the Lord spoke, "I reserve you totally for myself. Do
you prefer this reading that distracts you? Do I not give you all
that you need? I do not demand this strict sacrifice from others,
but you are my beloved. Even one instant away from me is too
much. My love does not rest."

Not Autosuggestion

In late August, the Lord said much but his messages melted together and I cannot put them into words. A great depression came over me. "Adorable Jesus, I do not have the strength to go to Church tonight." He replied, "Good. I will come to you." The next day, when I told this to the religious sister, she said, "This might be autosuggestion." Sadness and insecurity filled my soul. That night in Church, I asked, "My Jesus, was it just my imagination that you were with me? I do not know how to bring about autosuggestion."

The Lord responded, "Be still. This is a supernatural process. I come close to you to give you strength to make sacrifices. Nothing comes from your imagination."

The Loneliness of Jesus

On September 3 the Lord said, "All must do their part in my saving work. In many souls, this call is sleeping. They must awaken and not be lazy. I bothered you at the time of your rest, but no one else is around and I needed to pour out my troubles. My little sister, serve me."

Back on June 13, 1964, the Lord had breathed on me and said, "Only a thin veil, like a breath, separates us from one another. This fine veil is your bodily life that keeps you captive on earth." When I write that the Lord is near or in front of me, I do not see Him. However, He allows me to experience His presence. I explain this to avoid misunderstandings.

Later, on September 14, the Lord said, "Come, just come. I can hardly wait for your arrival. Your sacrifices are more numerous. You make me happy. Believe me. Everyone has the power to make God happy."

The Terrifying Doubts

The Evil One disoriented me and I could stand it no more. I went to the religious sister and confessed that I was a liar. She responded, "I do not believe that you want to deceive me." This did not calm me down.

The next day I went to confess my doubts. At first, my director did not recognize my voice. Then, he did not grasp what was happening. I said that this torment is not new. I do not even receive Communion. Father tried to calm me down, "Go to Communion. I take responsibility. You commit no sin." He said the Evil One was trying to push me into despair. His words calmed me but when I left the confessional, the evil spirits burst upon me a hundredfold, saying that I misled my confessor and that my lies are even more serious. I drew near to the Virgin, "My Mother, cover my sins so your Son is not saddened by me."

Two days later, the Lord said, "Put your earthly things in order. Time passes quickly and you fly to me without sensing the speed. Now, there is a great distance between you and earth. I await you."

The next day, the Lord explained, "After a period of relief, sufferings will again flood your soul. This is how it will be until your death. Just as night and day follow one another, so light and darkness will replace one another in your soul. I do not allow the night to rule continuously and I do not want you to enjoy continual light. This is how it must be."

Breaking the Fast

I keep the strict fast on Monday to free priestly souls from purgatory. However, I was so weak from sorrow that hunger came over me. I could not resist and I ate some food. I experienced great pain because I could not help the priestly soul to be freed from purgatory. As my compassion grew, I asked the Lord what to do. He did not answer.

Finally, on the third day, the Blessed Virgin answered, "Pray the complete rosary and assist at mass for the priest. In this way, you will regain what you lost for this priest and his soul will come into God's presence." By Our Lady's kindness, peace returned.

The Lord's Goal

On the way to mass, my thoughts were distracted. The Lord said, "Do not let your thoughts wander. Think only of me. If I correct you, do not be distressed. I want you to be attentive. Even a minute is a long time, if you spend it on something else.

"Let no creature come between us. Write down my words so others realize that they can only possess God if they come far away from all earthly noise. You are a living proof that this is possible. I put you in a family setting so all can see that they can serve their family and God at the same time."

Wasting Time

On October 9, the Lord said, "I complain to you so you can tell my complaints to others. I am so disappointed. What hurts most is that consecrated souls set me aside. They have no time to spend with me. They give their time to other things. You foolish ones. every minute passes. The time you spend on me is never lost. It is saved for eternity. Since you will render an account of how you spend your time, why not do everything for me. This is so easy."

Explaining Divine Mysteries

On October 16 the Lord said, "I pour over you the light of the divine mysteries." When I tried to express these mysteries in words, the Lord said, "Do not try anymore. All would be in vain. I have placed some drops of divine mysteries in your soul, like water into wine. You cannot separate out these drops of water and you cannot explain divine mysteries."

Vatican Council II

On October 25 the Lord promised, "Once Satan is blinded, the decrees of Vatican Council II will be fulfilled in an extraordinary way." (The Council had begun two weeks earlier.)

A Devout Life Without Sacrifice

On October 30 the Lord surprised me, "How happy I am that you assist at various masses. This honors me greatly. Tell all that the mass is a manifestation of my presence and I pour out great graces through the mass."

For many days in early November, the Lord lamented, "I have serous complaints against pious souls who make no sacrifices. They hurt my heart. Their devout life does not assure them of the merits needed to gain eternal salvation. Many act as if they were afraid to come close to me. Write to the indifferent soul, 'There is no progress without sacrifice.' I do not want sterile devotion, like a tree that bears no fruit. Grace only illumines hearts that are burning.

"I speak in a severe tone of voice. Pious souls must take my words to heart. O fools, you do not know how your pious indifference causes me immense sorrow. Repent! Repent! Repent! All of you, repent. Only the voice of repentance holds back my Father's chastising hand. On the way to Calvary, I asked the pious women to be sorry for their sins, not for me."

On November 13, the Lord promised, "I have given great light to your confessor. He sees clearly the road that he must take to put Our Cause into action. We have gained one of the Twelve." I saw that Satan was blind and realized all the good effects coming to mankind. As I fell asleep, my guardian angel woke me up. "How can you sleep with a great joy that will shake the world?" The Lord explained, "Satan being blind signifies a worldwide triumph of my Sacred Heart, the freedom of souls and a full opening of the road of salvation."

Our Lady reminded me that I forgot to kiss my scapular before going to bed.

Not Touching Her Lips

On November 18, when I received Communion, the Lord spoke about the host, "I yearn so much to be with you that I fly into your heart without touching your lips." The next day, the same experience happened. The host did not touch my lips but flew into my soul.

The Lord promised, "After your death, your neighbors will receive abundantly from your treasures. They will follow your simple road of life. My graces remain in your soul because you have dug a great channel by your sacrifices. Many souls receive abundant graces but they are not prepared for them and the graces drain out. I will stop complaining and I will prepare you."

A Heavenly Experience

I do not know what happened to me. I remember the noonday bell announcing the Angelus and the noisy announcements on the radio but I do not remember anything else all day. All I can write is that it was a great sacrifice to return to earthly life.

The Great Trials

In December, the great spiritual trials returned. The Lord explained, "Accept everything for my glory. The suffering will end up in my glory. When you leave earth, you will enjoy this glory."

The anguish increased and was accompanied by doubts of faith. For a few moments, the Lord calmed the distress by saying, "I hope that your sacrificial suffering never ends. To the extent that you experience doubts and anguish, to that extent light and relief will come upon others. Suffer with heroism. From time to time, I will lift the veil and show you my joy."

The Power of The Flame of Love

On December 6, Our Blessed Mother surprised me, "With your help I will perform a miracle that the intellectuals will try to imitate in vain. It will never be in their power.

"We will put out fire with fire. Satan's hatred hurls its flames so high that he believes victory is secure. But, my Flame of Love will blind Satan. I have given this Flame into your hands. Soon, it will arrive at its destination and will quench the fire of hell. Satan's fire burns in some minds and hearts. I want my gentle Flame to burn there, instead. As the number who sacrifices increases, the Flame will grow greater. The brilliance of my Flame of Love will fill the whole earth."

The Mystical Experiences

The Lord's graces were so intense I could hardly walk. Let no one be surprised by this. When this experience happens, the Lord's grace burns within my soul. Even others experience what is happening within me. However, not everyone experiences these graces equally. The experience varies according to their merits.

On December 12, on the way to mass, the Lord spoke, "Your soul is like the pure water of a lake and my divine eyes can see what is within you. The pebbles at the bottom are your sins, but now they shine with light because of your repentance.

"You could not walk because of my gaze, which has reached a new level. My Elizabeth, I long for you to come to heaven. Our union on earth has reached a level that you desire martyrdom. My soul rejoiced because of your willingness to suffer. According to your promptness, the Holy Cause will make progress. Your martyrdom prepares for the success of the messages and My graces will quickly triumph in souls."

All morning, as I did my household chores, it was as if I was not living on earth. I was possessed by the presence of Our Lord and Our Lady. By God's favor, I am fully immersed in the knowledge of my nothingness. This is the Lord's greatest favor.

Three Parts

The Lord said he would divide my life into three parts, pain and suffering, strengthening graces and ecstasies, and the spiritual dryness that I will experience as I return to earthly life.

Chapter Five

1965

As the year began, Our Lady spoke, "By my Flame of Love, I will place the crown of success on the Holy Council" (Vatican II was completed in December, 1965).

The Great Spiritual Darkness

By mid-January, I was in spiritual darkness, believing that all had been my imagination and pure lies. In spite of my efforts, I came under this power. This anguish was increased by doubts against faith. My confused thoughts convinced me that all was evil. This insecurity led to a violent hopelessness. So, I decided that I must end my continual lies. Otherwise, I will be condemned.

I thought, "I do not want to sin, so I will rip out these lies. I will leave all behind. I will not speak with anyone who knows me. I will never go to my confessor. He is too easy on me. I will not write the Lord's words anymore. They are my own invention. I wrote under the impulse of pride."

When I stopped writing these words, a new fear overpowered me—that I was not fulfilling the Lord's request. I was entrapped in torments, and I even abandoned the fight for a short time. The Lord spoke but I thought his words were just the effect of my lies. I heard the Blessed Virgin sobbing in my soul but I took this as my own imagination.

Attempts To Be Free

I live now in a terrible spiritual world, trying to free myself. In vain, I asked the bishop, Father X and Father D to free me from evil spirits. They calmed me down, hoping that God would make things clear. So, I just continued in my lies. I asked my confessor to be strict with me because I felt he was too kind. My confessions brought no relief. The priest did not see my lies. Due to my unrest, I did not go to confession.

My feelings were always changing. The battle was unbearable. For years, I have been suffering this. O happy death. If the good God leaves me in purgatory until Judgment Day, I will gladly accept it. In purgatory, I cannot sin.

Date of Death

(At some point, the Lord revealed to Elizabeth the date of her death.) When I heard the date that I would die and be among the blessed, I was filled with thanksgiving. I will go to a new confessor and mention nothing about the Cause. My previous confessions were filled with pretense. I am living with terrible torments.

I went to confession and found great relief for two or three days. Really, I was captivated by happiness and could not contain it. I was at the Carmelite convent and wanted all the sisters to experience this ecstasy. I kissed the forehead of the sister companion. She experienced the effect of this grace in my soul. The Lord spoke, "The eye of God rests upon you."

The Lord's Assurance

On February 4, the Lord spoke and peace entered my soul. This gave me an unmistakable strength. The Lord said, "Satan, deprived of light, could not lead you into sin. A fierce anger overwhelmed him because you will bring about my holy will. He wanted to blot this task out of your mind. Many will oppose these messages and you will suffer for the Cause. Explain the state of your soul to your confessor."

A Special Story

On February 14, while at Church, the Lord reminded me, "Leave now. You must buy bread for your family." However, the store was out of bread. As I was leaving, they said someone had called and ordered bread but did not pick it up. The Lord said, "I ordered the bread for you. Time given to me never harms the family."

Experiences of Ecstasies

On April 7, I told the religious sister that it seems the Lord had abandoned me. At home, the Lord said, "Why do you think I am so far away? Really, I stand next to you." Then, I felt Our Lady's love and heard her say, "She is my special one, also." Our Lady was so immersed in the Trinity, that I could hardly distinguish her. I wondered how Jesus allowed me to experience this. He explained, "This is just a form of ecstasy which even your bodily powers can experience." Then, the Lord initiated me into heavenly experiences that I cannot write about.

On Monday of Holy Week, the Lord said, "Many do not see my hand begging for help. I draw close but they turn away and keep walking the road of darkness. The Flame of Love will be placed on earth to enlighten these souls.

"My Mother wants the oil of your sacrifices to fall on the lamps of souls. I promise that whenever you pray for someone you will never be refused. When souls make sacrifices for my saving work, I am in debt to them. They buy me with their favors."

The Doctor's Report

In May, I went back to the doctor who had done laboratory tests. The results showed that I had a little anemia, which was totally insignificant. He detected no sickness and prescribed no medication.

His only explanation was that I accepted the sufferings of others. My nervous system is very sensitive and this causes sufferings. He had no other answer. My children know that I am always in a poor state of health and were greatly surprised by the doctor's evaluation. They found this strange. I just suffered (as usual).

The Repeated Miracle of the Holy Spirit

On May 15, the Lord said, "Do not grow indecisive in this despairing state. You must undergo the same sufferings as my disciples after my death. In this way, I can send the Holy Spirit. The great miracle is the repeated coming of the Holy Spirit. His light will spread over and penetrate the whole earth." After the Lord finished, dark suffering again filled my soul.

Five days later the Lord surprised me, "Be strong. I will not give you any more sufferings." I was saddened and complained, "How can I come before you? Your love dominates my soul. What will happen to me? Why do you treat me this way? Do I not merit sufferings?"

He spoke again, "You did not understand. I cannot increase your sufferings because you have reached the limit. There is no room for increased sufferings. I will not lessen your sufferings, nor will I spare you. You will suffer until your last breath."

Work in Heaven

On May 30, Our Lady said, "After your death, you will be next to me and the oil of your sacrifices will fall upon the lamps of earth. These will be lit again by the Flame of Love. They will fall upon those who have no lamp (unbelievers). They, too, will come to my Son. You will have work even in heaven."

The Lord Explains the Suffering

On June 10, before mass, the Lord said, "Experience the light of my penetrating glance. With this I give you a special strength.

I will never diminish your sufferings, but I will change their forms. That you are still living on earth is one form of suffering.

"I placed you under the full dominion of the Prince of Darkness. He could put you to any test to make you hesitate or withdraw. In this way, he knows he is confronting a soul possessed by the Holy Trinity. This kind of soul knows how to love and suffer in total conformity to the Divine Will. You are a victim burning with love. I keep you on earth so you can be this burning victim. I look upon you with favor."

My soul enjoyed peace, but only for a few days.

The Great Battle

Soon, an infuriating battle arose within. This was caused by my lies by which I dazzle myself. Not one word is true. I have so many sins that I do not receive Communion. I come to the same conclusion. I must destroy all my lies. I will not write one more word.

Even though I heard the Lord's voice within, I did not write and tried to leave all behind. I never experienced a torment like this. This is a terrible life. I know I am offending God and He has no desire to come to me. In this torment, I only want to die. Then I will be free of my lies that confuse even my confessors. I have no purpose. I am living without God. I only go to mass on Sunday. I nourish my soul by spiritual communions. All is dark. Life is strange for me. How can I live for God without having God?

Only the Holy Father can restore my peace. If he finds that the Cause is not true, he can absolve me. With the little strength I have, I will go to the Holy Father because I cannot just go on and do nothing. I will not continue to live this way. Either what is happening is true or I am a fool and a liar. If it is true, I cannot just stand around while souls are perishing. I must make whatever sacrifice is needed.

The Lord's Intervention

In July, the Lord spoke, "Your confessor told you to call him if you had any difficulty." So, I called him on the phone and his words were encouraging. That night, I was like a child waiting for Christmas day, because I would receive Communion tomorrow. For two weeks, I had not received. The favorable response had calmed my spiritual torments.

When I went to confession, the Evil One burst in again. I needed strength to listen to the priest. Several times, I had to say, "I want to believe that the absolution is valid." The priest understood. He showed me that the harassment comes from the Evil One. He strongly advised me, "Never stay away from Communion." I said, "yes" seven times to his repeated commands. To do this, I received a power greater than anything on earth.

The Lord's Explanation

A few days later, the Lord said, "Concerning your confessor's advice, I say again, 'His word is my word' because I enlighten him. He knows you, guides you, and will never abandon you. Did I not tell you that I would release Satan upon you? I rejoice that you went immediately to your confessor. You had this instrument of obedience and you diligently used this power."

Until today, I did not think about the greatness of obedience. I resolved to accept both the words of the Lord and those of my confessor.

The Night Vigil

On July 9, Our Lady said, "Give your confessor the instructions concerning the night vigils. These night vigils will save the souls of the dying and must be organized in every parish so someone is praying every moment. This is the instrument I place in your hands. Use it to blind Satan and to save the souls of the dying from eternal condemnation."

Three days later, the Lord promised, "I take one more step. I will honor your little dwelling with my continual presence. It will be my continual sanctuary. I have rented your little house. I see that you resist against believing my promise. From this, you know that the words are from me. What would you be without my love?"

The Fire of Charity—A Burning Arrow

On July 17 the Lord explained, "You regained peace only through obedience to the confessor's command. If you had rejected his word, your soul would have been shipwrecked once and for all. My words are serious. Your confessor's words are my words. To reject them is to revolt against God. Now, I will change your sufferings. Until the end of your life, the Fire of Charity will burn in you and consume the strength of your body."

Since the Lord had not yet given me this "Fire of Charity," I did not understand. After a few days, I felt as if a burning arrow had been thrust into my soul. By this suffering, souls will be saved from eternal fire. After experiencing it, I still cannot describe it. If even natural combustion is impossible to explain, how can I describe this "Flame of Charity"?

A Mystical Experience

A silent withdrawal dominates my soul. I feel like I am not on earth. The Lord said this would happen until the end of my life. I must be more faithful to the fasts and night vigils. I wanted to double these. Previously, the Lord asked me for two holy hours. After the Fire of Charity burned within me, I had no night and day. I pray from midnight to 5:00 AM. Then I go to Church. At 7:00 AM, I receive the Lord's Sacred Body. At home, my soul is joined to the Lord without interruption. These are the secrets of my heart.

Effects of the Fire of Charity

The bodily weakness diagnosed by the doctor comes with such intensity that I must lie down for 15 minutes every hour. Returning from mass, the weakness came and I had to lie down. The Lord poured his Fire of burning charity in the greatest measure, while saying, "God has come down to you." My soul shook intensely for a long time.

Our Lady said, "God has come down to you and the fire of burning charity consumes you. To possess this privilege you need great humility."

I often feel a great inhibition about writing. This paralyzes me for days. Then, the Lord grows firm and demands that I write these things. He said, "Why do I make you write about these things? These events reflect my grace. I oblige you to write, so all will see what I have done in you since your infancy."

The Lord's Assurances

The Lord had said to me. "I cannot give you up." Today, he explained, "Why are you surprised? I shed all the drops of my blood to save everyone. With all your strength, you must want the same thing, that everyone be saved."

Because the Fire of Charity now inflames me, I experience ecstasy much more frequently and in unexpected moments. I am in so much pain that I could not pray for the dying. The Lord assured me that He accepted my "desire to pray." Those were the words he used.

Infused Vitality

Two grandchildren were born August 22 (Immaculate heart of Mary) and September 8 (Birthday of Mary). The work of caring for them was too much and I asked for strength. The next day I had amazing vitality and for two weeks, I experienced no tiredness. I even thought of going back to work. Then, the

Lord spoke, "You understand now why I stripped you of bodily strength. In your weakness, you served me. In your strength, you give me less time and do not stay with me. This strength will remain just a few days. I gave it for the good of your family."

Hesitancy About A Request

On September 18, the Lord asked me to fast on bread and water until the Cause reaches the Holy Father. He returned a few days later and repeated his request. However, due to my weak strength, I did not think that I could fulfill it. Yet, it was clearly the Lord's will. The Fire of Charity burns within and I want only what the Lord wants. Usually, I decide quickly but now I went back and forth. Only by the seventh day did I accept the Lord's will.

However, when I went to my confessor, he refused to allow it. I felt at peace for a few days until the Lord spoke, "I do not withdraw my request. Go to your confessor and ask again." I was confused and told the Lord of his refusal. I returned again and gave him the Lord's request. He again refused and showed me how absurd it was. He rejected it because it would hurt my health and violated the fifth commandment. If the Lord told him, he would grant it immediately.

After that, however, whenever I thought about food, dizziness came over me. This ceased when I had bread and water. The Lord said I should eat other foods only at lunch. I was to eat only to feed my body, and not to enjoy the taste. On Monday and Thursday, I live on bread and water. I do likewise on Friday, only taking food after 6:00 PM. If I took other food on those days, I would suffer.

The Lord kept asking me to renew his request to my confessor. "I want you to fulfill my request until the petitions reach the Holy Father. Tell your confessor that I change your sufferings and he should not be afraid. No matter how often I send you, you must go promptly.

"However, never disobey the commands of your confessor, not even for my divine request. If your confessor had accepted my request, your sacrifices would have gained the intended result. He would have received the needed strength to make sure that the Cause arrived at the Holy Father."

Experiencing Transubstantiation

In October, when the priest said the words of consecration and elevated the host, the Lord allowed me to experience the transubstantiation of his Body. He said, "To experience this sublime moment in your soul is the work of special graces of divine love." My soul trembled and I thought, "When the apostles first experienced the miracle of transubstantiation with the Lord, how could they stand it?" In these few moments, I felt as if I was going to die. Even now, these effects are difficult to accept.

Sufferings and Ecstasy

The Lord Jesus flooded me with extraordinary sufferings. I was bent over when I walked, and a fear of death took hold of me. The Lord said, "Do not grow tired of these sufferings." Gradually, the sufferings lessened and the Lord said, "Suffer with a smile. Let no one know and let no one see. This is our secret." At that moment, I felt as if my soul separated from my body.

Many times, the Lord said, "Sorrow for your sins produces bank interest here on earth." A light bathed my soul in indescribable happiness. His longing for souls burned with a fire that constantly grew within me.

On December 17, after Communion, the Lord filled me with light and said, "My light penetrates you and is all around you. You must give light to the dark parts of the earth."

Chapter Six

1966

On January 3, I experienced a profound sorrow for sins. The Lord's words left a living mark on my soul, "Repentance has immense power. Sometimes, my hand is raised to punish. Then, those who make reparation force me to pardon."

Repentance and Ecstasy

On January 13, after Holy Communion, the Lord spoke, "Your repentance touches my heart. I will imprint a brilliant sign of pure gold on your soul which you merited by constant repentance. Even after your death, it will shine with light and will radiate the gift of repentance to others. You are a good and blessed soul."

While the sound of the Lord's words were still ringing in my ears, my soul left earth. He added, "I only lift purified souls up to Myself."

Lighting Up the World

Three days later, I lit a match to make a fire. The Lord surprised me, "You are like this match and I have lit you. You will light up the whole world. You are a small instrument, but with one strike of the match, I will enkindle the Flame of Love in millions of souls. Satan's fire cannot extinguish this flame. My Mother will light one match and blind him."

Divine Experiences

On February 25, at night, I got off the bus but could hardly walk in the snowy street. I was alone and fearful. The Lord surprised me, "Why do you consider yourself alone? I will never let go of you." The experience grew stronger as he spoke, "Long ago, even when you did not think of me, I was with you. I followed you at every step. Reject every idea that you are alone. If, for one instance, you do not think of me, my suffering becomes great. Is there anything that you want?"

I responded, "Lord, before all else, I desire souls for you."

The next day at morning mass, the Lord brought me into ecstasy. In this experience, I do not see. I just hear the Lord's words. Taking full possession of my soul he said, "We are bringing you the most beautiful gift of our hearts." In these moments of ecstasy, the Lord Jesus gave me his heart and soul. I experienced the Divine Heart beating within me. Everything else, I cannot write. I participate in the infinite goodness of God.

On March 4 our conversation lasted all morning while I was doing my work. I listen carefully to every word, "On the chords of your soul I play a melody of repentance. This comes from your sufferings. The melody falls upon sinners, and even the obstinate repent."

Defining Her Task

A few weeks later the Lord defined my task. "You are the prompter in the divine drama. The prompter has no need to know the names of the audience. He makes the show go well. He is not the star and does not appear on stage. He experiences no peace. He is always on the move. This is your position. Give yourself totally. Do whatever needs to be done. This is enough. I never seek results."

The Daily Miracle

The next day, the Lord's presence traveled across my body and soul. I am in such pain from those who reject graces and face the terrible danger of eternal condemnation. At Holy Communion, as the Lord Jesus enters my soul, a profound silence overwhelms me and his words resound in my ears. At the moment of divine union, my every stirring is one with God. This miracle happens every day.

A Promise of Heaven

On Good Friday (April 9), while I adored the cross, the Lord said, "Only my Mother can understand the mystery of the Word made Flesh. Other souls understand this only through sufferings. I say to you what I said to the Good Thief, 'The day of your death, you will be with me in Paradise.'" As I write these words, the beating of Our Lord's heart forced me to my knees.

Locutions After Easter

After Easter, the Lord spoke on many occasions. On April 14 I wondered how I could repay God. Being a daring person, I said, "Lord, I will repay you with sorrow for my sins." The Lord said, "I have already bought your sins but I will use your repentance to pay for others. Your repentance will enkindle perfect sorrow in a multitude of souls."

On another occasion, the Lord said, "You comprehend divine mysteries because, during your ecstasies, I teach you these mysteries to strengthen you to suffer."

One day, I said, "Adorable Jesus, you are the child of my eyes." He responded, "You say this so rarely. Because of my human nature, I like to be pampered."

One morning, the Lord said "Every tear that suffering draws from your eyes will bring forth tears of repentance in sinners."

On June 3 I said to Our Lady, "Until you give my confessor your requests, he will do nothing." She answered, "My Flame of Love makes no exceptions. I will flood him with the gentle light, which he cannot resist. I will do the same for all who are called to pass along the Flame. The purer the soul, the more fully my Flame of Love will shine."

A few days later, at the altar, the Lord revealed my poverty of soul and spoke, "I cover over this poverty so others will see only the richness radiating from your soul. I have made you the distributor of my graces."

Chapter Seven

The Final Years

From 1967 to her death in 1985, Elizabeth recorded relatively little in her Spiritual Diary.

A Promise

On November 7, 1969, while adoring the Holy Trinity, I heard the Lord speak, "Soon, I will send you a priest who will take your soul and Our Holy Cause into his hands."

You Must Speak

On July 26, 1971 the Lord said, "Speech is a gift of God and, one day, all must give an account of their words. We cannot wrap ourselves in silence. You must use this gift that the Father gave you. Do not be afraid to speak! You must shake people and awaken them from their lethargy. You cannot leave them with empty hands and empty hearts. You must speak!"

Then, Our Lady taught me, "You must explain my Flame of Love by speaking about it. You have no right to be silent because of cowardice, pride, or negligence. Let your words be alive and have an impact. Ask for a word and I will give it. Each word is a seed planted in the listeners that will bring forth a harvest."

Again, the Lord spoke, "Get the inactive and fearful priests to leave their homes. They must not stand idle and deprive humanity of my Mother's Flame of Love. They must speak out so I can pour out my pardon on the whole world.

"Go into battle. Satan tries to ruin the good. Christians cannot be satisfied with little efforts, here or there. Trust my Mother. The world of the future is being prepared. The smile of my Mother will light up the whole earth."

Four Teachings

On July 11, 1975 Elizabeth recorded four teachings.

First Teaching

Our Lady spoke, "Many are blinded by material things. They cannot come closer to God because material goods are a wall. Even well intentioned souls only make sacrifices from time to time. Blinded by earthly goods and desires, they cannot receive special graces. They do not follow God's inspirations, and do not want to believe that God will lead them.

Second Teaching

Our Lord spoke, "People make donations but they want their name listed. This remembrance is for their own glory. Give your donations anonymously and the heavenly Father will reward you."

Third Teaching

The Flame of Love prepares our souls for the Lord's inspirations. If we depend on the Flame of Love, the Lord will enlighten our intellect and show us the most perfect will of God.

Fourth Teaching

The heavenly Father says that in the measure that we love God, the world will be freed from sin. We are responsible for one another, for our family and our nation. Feel responsible for the fate of all humanity. Our Lady said, "All will see the results of their labors on behalf of the Flame of Love."

Destroying the Writings

The following is not a part of the Spiritual Diary. It is a letter, written by Elizabeth to a close friend, Doctor N.

Because of doubts, I came to know that what I had written did not come from God. To be free, I decided to destroy the material (which now has many volumes) by burning it in the stove in my little dwelling. As I was about to throw the writings in the fire, the Lord paralyzed my hand. The messages fell on the floor and I collapsed. My daughter, Cecilia, found me. She understood what I was doing and took the writings to her room in the house. I ran after her and retrieved them.

I again knelt before the stove and again my hand was paralyzed. I could not act and realized I was doing wrong. The Lord wanted the messages given to the world.

In spring 1971 I was in total darkness from grave doubts. I asked the Lord to scatter my confusion. "O Lord, if this Cause is authentic, then why must I live in darkness?" I collapsed and began to bang my fist on the furniture. "I seek a sign so I can withstand these torments." With total lack of respect, I demanded a sign from God (this even made me laugh). I asked God for what he certainly cannot give me. I demanded that a certain priest come to my dwelling by noontime. If so, I would accept the Cause as authentic. After issuing this challenge, I felt very good.

When I went to Church, I was covered with shame. I went to confession and told the priest of my disrespectful dispute with God. He reproved me, told me I was a "hard head" and, for my penance, I was to pray for my own conversion. This priest is a tough person. I did speak up, "Wouldn't you discuss things with God if you suffered my torments?" I prayed for myself. "O God, convert this hard-head."

The darkness lifted and, after mass, I went home totally forgetting what had happened. As the noon bells rang, a knock came to my dwelling. It was the priest whom I had sought as a sign. "Who sent you and why did you come?" I asked. "No one sent me. I just felt some need to come immediately." I told him what happened. Also, the "hard head" returned to God.

Doubts and Crises

In 1977, as the doubts came upon me, I decided to retract the message. I went to the twelve Hungarian priests, "Do not believe what I told you. They are lies that I invented." I hid nothing and revealed my terrible torments.

This great moment of Calvary arrived when I went before my confessor and all the other priests. The response I remember most came from one priest, "Because the Lord Jesus spoke to you again after you retracted the messages, there is no reason to be ashamed. We are face to face with God's will." (End of Letter)

The Monday Fast

On August 15, 1980, the Blessed Virgin asked the priests, consecrated souls, and anyone else who was able, to fast on Mondays on bread and water. She promised, "If priests observe this Monday fast in all the holy masses that they celebrate that week, at the moment of Consecration, they will free innumerable souls from Purgatory." (Elizabeth asked how many were meant by innumerable. The Lord responded, "So many that it cannot be expressed in human numbers.") "Consecrated souls and the faithful who keep the Monday fast will free a multitude of souls each time they receive Communion that week."

The Lord said, "The Church and the whole world are in danger. You cannot change this situation. Only the Holy Trinity, through the unified intercession of the Blessed Virgin, the angels, the saints and the souls in purgatory, can help you."

Explaining the Fast

Our Lady explained the fast. We can eat abundant bread, with salt. We can take vitamins, medicines, and what we need for health. We can drink abundant water. We should not eat to enjoy. Whoever keeps the fast should do so until at least 6:00 PM. In this case, they should recite five decades of the rosary for holy souls.

Prayer Communities

On January 1, 1981, Our Lord said, "Go beyond your limits. Look at the three Wise Men who made superhuman efforts. Especially priests must act this way. Others should do likewise. We must intensify prayer. We must sacrifice for world peace and for the salvation of souls. We must go to the limit. Every parish must urgently form Communities of prayer. Bless each other with the sign of the cross."

Our Lady said that the sign of the cross expels Satan, as does the ejaculatory prayer "Spread the effect of the grace of thy Flame of love over all of humanity."

Carmelite Third Order

In the spring (1981), Our Lady asked me to speak with the authorities to have the Third Order of Carmelites restored throughout the world. Humanity needs secular people with a spirit of prayer. While Our Lady spoke about Carmel, the Lord interrupted, "My Mother is Noah's Ark." He often said this. Our Lady also said, "From Hungary, I want this Flame put into action. Humanity must fulfill my request."

On April 12, she repeated her words, "All who delay this outpouring of grace have a grave responsibility." These words weighed heavily upon me. The Lord spoke, "Do not fear. We are with you. Just do not delay."

Then, both spoke together, "Through you, we ask for a great mobilization of the whole world. Multitudes in every part of the world should petition the Holy Father (Pope John Paul II) for an official declaration of the effusion of the Flame of Love of Our Hearts for the whole world. We do not ask the Holy Father to examine this. That will take too long. Everyone just needs to experience this in his or her own heart. Our petition is urgent. No time for delays. Let priests and their people gather in spiritual oneness. This outpouring will reach even the souls of the non-baptized."

The diary ends with Our Lady's petition, "My children, pray for one another without ceasing. Let the outpouring of my graces produce its effect in souls."

Translator's Personal Contribution

After months of being immersed in translating the Spiritual Diary, I would like to make a personal contribution to The Cause, as Our Lord and Our Lady so often called this work. There is no need to clarify this book. The words are very easy to understand. I would like to point out what is central in this diary.

Elizabeth Kindelmann

She is a remarkable woman, in every aspect of her life. She did not allow being an orphan to destroy her. At 33, she became a widow with six young children in a Hungary that was controlled by Communism. She often worked two jobs in factories at low wages to support her family.

She suffered through the mystical dark nights without a spiritual guide. At 49 (1962), when Our Lord and Our Lady entrusted the great Cause to her, she was alone and tried to convince priests that these messages came from heaven. The Lord had deliberately kept her away from any formal schooling to prove that this Diary had a divine source.

In the course of her diary, she describes all the mystical favors received by the great saints, even though she doesn't know the names of the favors. She experiences ecstasy, flights of the spirit, and divine absorption. With all of these favors, she remains totally humble.

Her ascent to God is always accompanied by greater sufferings. Jesus would remove one type of torment, only to substitute greater burdens. These sufferings were in her body, her emotions, her mind, and her soul. Nothing is spared yet she is filled with great joy. Some day, she will certainly be canonized. I hope that will not scratch away her many human elements.

Unlike Saint Margaret Mary and Saint Faustina, Elizabeth never enjoyed a vision of our Lord or Our Lady. She wrote that the Lord was sitting next to her, but then carefully noted that she "did not see him but felt his presence." She enjoyed what St. John of the Cross describes as "locutions," and the bulk of her diary records these words very carefully.

The Cause

In these locutions, Jesus and Mary speak frequently and urgently about "the Cause," Elizabeth's task to "put the Cause into action," in other words, "to get it moving." A very important question is, "Just what is this Cause?" I will try to answer that from my own immersion in the Diary.

The heart and center of the Cause is the "Flame of Love of Our Lady's heart."

This Flame of Love is the greatest grace God has given the world since "the Word became Flesh."

The purpose of this Flame is "to blind Satan" so he loses control over souls. These souls will regain their freedom, so they can choose eternal life.

The central goal is the salvation of every soul in the world.

Another important effect is the freeing of souls from purgatory.

Although all these tremendous graces will come from the Flame of Love, people must know about this Flame and how they are expected to respond. This is The Cause.

What Is Expected

The devotion has a special prayer: "Spread the effect of grace of Thy Flame of Love over all of humanity."

People should say this as an ejaculatory prayer. However, Our Lady wants this prayer inserted into the Hail Mary after the phrase, "pray for us sinners."

The center of Flame of Love is adoration before the Blessed Sacrament. The diary stresses a nighttime hour, when normally no one is there.

Our Lord wants someone adoring the Blessed Sacrament in every parish Church at every hour. Our Lady promises that no one who dies in the parish while someone is adoring will be condemned.

The devotion asks for a Family holy hour.

The devotion includes a strict fast (bread and water) every Monday until 6:00 PM.

Thursday and Fridays are also days of strict fast until 6:00 PM.

Prayer Groups

People are encouraged to receive the Flame and pass it on. The important means to accomplish this is the forming of parish or home prayer groups.

Abandonment to God

Intertwined with these prayers and sacrifices, is the spirit of belonging totally to God. All that is not of God and which absorbs the human heart must be removed.

By grace, Elizabeth was able to do this. At the same time, she was deeply involved in raising her children and caring for her grandchildren, most of whom moved back into her house. She lived in a little room in her garden.

Please, do not be overwhelmed. Our Lady does not expect the average lay person to suddenly reach these spiritual heights. Many sufferings and spiritual favors are unique to Elizabeth. The Diary is not systematic. It describes Elizabeth's many struggles. As you read the Diary, you will see, as I did, many little things that you can easily do now. The Diary will get inside you. When it does, you will discover that Our Lady has placed her Flame of Love in your heart. If you persevere, you will experience all the blessings. Which God intends for you.

May the Flame of Love be lit in your heart!

Questions and Answers

Hopefully, this section will clarify the main aspects of the Flame of Love devotion. The National Center hopes to provide more explanatory booklets.

Why do we need this new devotion?

Our Lady, by her intercession, has gained from the heavenly Father the greatest graces in the history of the world since the Father sent His Son, Jesus Christ, into the world. This new devotion alerts the world to these new graces and instructs us how to receive them.

What is the Flame of Love?

The Flame is Jesus Christ himself. He is the gift of the Father. God uses this image because we can easily perceive ourselves receiving a flame and passing it on.

What is the main prayer of this devotion?

The most important is the ejaculatory prayer, "Spread the effect of grace of thy Flame of Love over all of humanity." Our Lady asked that this petition be added to the Hail Mary after "pray for us sinners."

Besides the above the Lord gave to her the following prayer as an effective weapon against Satan:

May our feet journey together.

May our hands gather in unity.

May our hearts beat in unison.

May our souls be in harmony.

May our thoughts be as one.

May our ears listen to the silence together.

May our glances profoundly penetrate each other.

May our lips pray together to gain mercy from the Eternal Father.

The Lord told her that this prayer will blind Satan and souls will not be led into sin.

What are the purposes of this devotion?

The primary purpose is that every soul be saved. Another clear purpose is that souls in Purgatory go to heaven as soon as possible. These two goals are highlighted in the many promises. Our Lady also promises to blind Satan.

What does it mean "to blind Satan"?

Whenever he is given an opening, Satan spreads his influence into every aspect of everyone's life. His powers block God's graces and do not allow the person to turn to God, to repent, or to be freed. Blinding Satan means that he loses this power. Then, God's graces can be effective and the person can respond. For example, an active alcoholic is caught up in an addiction. Alcohol has power over him. By becoming a recovering alcoholic, he is free to fulfill his obligations. Alcohol no longer has power over him. So, when Satan is blinded, souls are free to respond to God's grace.

Is there any feast day for the Flame of Love?

Our Lady wanted no special feast day but she chose Candlemas Day (February 2) as the feast day for this devotion. Obviously, her choice was perfect.

Did Elizabeth have many experiences?

She had agony and ecstasy and she records these as clearly as possible, obviously being reluctant to describe the ecstasies.

What have Our Lord and Our Lady promised us through this devotion?

The promises are extraordinary and are scattered throughout the Diary. The greatest promise concerns a parish where people pray in holy hours of adoration. In that parish, no one who dies while someone is in adoration will be condemned. There are also promises of releasing souls from Purgatory, especially family members, when a person observes the Monday fast. A complete list of these promises is given below.

April 1962: The Monday fast on bread and water will free a priestly soul from Purgatory.

September 7, 1962: At night vigils, the Flame of Love will bless dying people all over the world as Satan will be blinded.

September 28, 1962: If a person fasts for a priest, the priest will be released from Purgatory eight days after his death.

November, 1965: Our Lady said, "If at any moment, someone prays three Hail Mary's in my honor, while referring to the Flame of Love, they will free a soul from purgatory.

During November, one Hail Mary will free ten souls."

March 27, 1963: Our Lord said, "The face of the earth will be renewed because something like this has not happened since the Word became Flesh. Earth will be renewed by Our Lady's intercession."

September 24, 1964: Our Lady promised, "If a family keeps a holy hour on Thursday or Friday, and if someone in that family dies, the person will be freed from Purgatory after one day of the fast by a family member."

December 2, 1963: Our Lady promised, "Through a few people, a great outpouring of graces will change the world. No one must refuse my invitation."

January 20, 1964: Our Lord promised, "Whoever reads about the graces I gave you yesterday, will share in these graces." (This was the grace of holy trembling, an experience which comes from an infusion of grace.)

December 6, 1964: Our Lady said, "The Flame of Love will quench the fire of hell and the Flame's brilliance will fill the whole earth."

What do Our Lord and Our Lady ask of us?

As individuals, they ask that:

We dedicate holy hours to adoration and reparation. This can be in the Church or at home.

Make little sacrifices for souls.

Be detached from worldly distractions.

Fast on bread and water on Monday and Thursday until 6:00 PM and on Fridays until 3:00 PM. On those days, we should say five decades of the rosary.

Speak always about the Flame of Love.

As a parish, they ask that:

Prayer communities be formed in every parish and that people are in 24 hour adoration. If so, they promise that no one in that parish who dies will be condemned (an extraordinary promise).

What is the function of the National Center?

We are just beginning (Fall, 2012). Right now we publish the entire Spiritual Diary (90,000 words) and this simplified Version (31,000 words). We hope to have more booklets explaining and encouraging the Movement. We will also act as a Communication Center, attempting to list Flame of Love activities and, eventually, to publish a newsletter. At this point, we would like to hear from you. Please make suggestions and tell us about the Flame of Love in your life and your parish.

Elizabeth Kindelmann

(1913 – 1985)

Elizabeth was the 13th child, born after six sets of twins, and the only one to survive to adulthood. By the time she was 5, both her parents had died. At 16, she married Karoly Kindelmann and had six children. At 32, she became a widow, with the superhuman task of providing for her family. At 48 (1961) Our Lord and Our Lady began to reveal this devotion to the Flame of Love of Mary's Immaculate Heart. Her easy-to-read diary reveals the rest of the story.

The Flame of Love of the Immaculate Heart of Mary

Learn how to:

- Receive this Flame of Love
- Experience the Effects of the Flame
- Pass the Flame to Others
- Blind Satan so that he has no power over you or your loved ones
- Save the dying in your parish from eternal condemnation
- Release many souls from purgatory

The Spiritual Diary of Elizabeth Kindelmann
Budapest, Hungary